By Fr. Sebastian Walshe, O. Praem.

SECRETS FROM HEAVEN

Hidden Treasures of Faith in the Parables and Conversations of Jesus

D1096901

Catholic
Answers
Press

Published by Catholic Answers, Inc.
2020 Gillespie Way
El Cajon, California 92020
1-888-291-8000 orders
619-387-0042 fax
catholic.com

Printed in the United States of America

Cover by Theodore Schluenderfritz
Interior by Russell Graphic Design

978-1-68357-168-1
978-1-68357-169-8 Kindle
978-1-68357-170-4 ePub

Let the word of Christ dwell in you richly (Col. 3:16).

CONTENTS

INTRODUCTION

Do you remember the first time you began to read the Bible? Perhaps it was an assignment when you were in Catholic school. Or maybe you are an adult and you started reading Scripture because you were searching for something.

I remember distinctly the first time I started reading the Bible. My mom converted from Judaism to Christianity, and so when I was eight years old a Bible suddenly appeared in our home. Though I understood very little of what I read, I was fascinated by the stories in Genesis and later by the stories in the Gospels. I have now been a priest for almost fifteen years, and I have read the Bible, especially the New Testament, countless times. Thanks be to God I understand more now than I did as a child; yet I still have the wonder and fascination at the word of God that I did when I was eight.

But this is not always the case for those who have read or listened to the Bible over and over during Mass or in their personal study. After a while, the old familiar verses can begin to appear stale: the same old stories, the same old words, and the same old homilies about them.

Even with God's word, familiarity can breed, if not contempt, at least a certain boredom.

It should not be that way. We can never exhaust the word of God, for in Christ "are hidden all the treasures of wisdom and knowledge" (Col. 2:3). Because the scriptures are proposed by Divine Wisdom, in each passage there is an inexhaustible source of spiritual nourishment to be found. The deeper we penetrate, the more there is to understand. Their

lessons are heavenly secrets that reveal themselves, one by
one, at the seeking.

St. John of the Cross expresses this truth admirably in one
of his writings about the riches found in the scriptures:

> Though holy doctors have uncovered many mysteries
> and wonders, and devout souls have understood them in
> this earthly condition of ours, yet the greater part still re-
> mains to be unfolded by them, and even to be understood
> by them. We must dig deeply in Christ. He is like a rich
> mine with many pockets containing treasures: however
> deep we dig we will never find their end or their limit.
> Indeed, in every pocket new seams of fresh riches are
> discovered on all sides.[1]

What St. John says about Christ, the incarnate Word of
God, is equally true about the written word of God. For
we come to know Christ through Scripture: "Ignorance of
Scripture is ignorance of Christ," as St. Jerome famously said.[2]

The aim of this modest book is to help give you new
eyes and ears so that you may read and hear the word of
God afresh. The reason we do not profit anew from every
reading of Scripture is often that we are only scratching the
surface rather than digging deeply. For to dig deeply, we
need *tools* for our minds and we need *strength* for our hearts.
We need to understand the methods for uncovering the
treasures hidden in the word of God, and we need a heart
disposed to receive and profit from the truths we uncover.

The Words of the Word

"All scripture is inspired by God and is useful for teaching, for
refutation, for correction, and for training in righteousness"
(2 Tim. 3:16). But although all Scripture is the word of God,

there seems to be a special power to the words of Jesus himself, and a special grace that flows from them. Something about the words of Jesus moves us more easily to conversion, to love, to hope in the midst of trials. We can imagine him standing before us addressing those words to us, speaking directly to our heart, so that the sentiments of the disciples on the road to Emmaus become our own: "Were not our hearts burning within us while he spoke to us on the way?" (Luke 24:32).

For this reason, we will focus in a special way on the words of Jesus found in his conversations and parables. Of course, it is easy enough to pick up a copy of the Gospels and read these conversations and parables. Some Bibles even print the words of Jesus in red ink to make them easier to find. But I hope this book will not only present the words of Jesus to you but will help you to learn how to read them in a new way. Throughout these meditations, I will draw upon the insights of the great spiritual writers and commentators upon the Gospels, especially the Fathers and Doctors of the Church. As with Mary, it can be truly said of them that they kept the word of God, pondering over it in their hearts (Luke 2:19; Luke 8:15; Luke 11:28).

It is essential, if you are to derive the greatest profit from this little book, that you pray while reading it; pray that you will have ears to hear and be transformed like Jesus' hearers were. Words on the page are dead unless they are enlivened by the Spirit in the heart of one who reads them.

Finally, an editorial note: for the most part I will use the English translation of the Gospels found in the current Lectionary, since this is likely to be the text most familiar to readers and because it is heard in the context of the sacred liturgy. Yet every translation has limitations. Therefore, in some places I will offer alternative translations when the Greek original needs clarification or further explanation.

CHAPTER 1

READING THE WORD OF GOD

The apostles and disciples of Jesus saw and heard the same man that the unbelieving scribes and Pharisees did. Both beheld the incarnate Word of God, but they responded very differently to the experience. The reason is that God does not do violence to our freedom when he reveals himself. He leaves us room to choose or reject him. A belief that is compelled or nearly compelled has very little worth for the believer. This is why the Gospels relate that Jesus did not entrust himself to those who believed merely because of his miracles (John 2:23–25). We want signs to give evidence that we can use to make our own judgments. But faith that stands upon our own judgment rather than upon complete trust in God is ultimately just faith in ourselves.

The same principle holds true in approaching the written word of God. Two people can read the same text, and one can come away a believer but the other an unbeliever. The scriptures do not compel our faith. God wants us to trust him first, so that our faith will be founded upon his mercy and power rather than upon ourselves. Yet once we have placed our trust in him, God right away rewards this trust with many signs that strengthen the faith of a believer.

This interplay between God and the one seeking to be certain of the truth of divine revelation comes out in a brief exchange between Jesus and the Jewish leaders: "The Jews answered and said to him, 'What sign can you show us for doing this?' Jesus answered and said to them, 'Destroy this temple and in three days I will raise it up'" (John 2:18–19). They ask for a sign in the present to make sure he is who he claims to be. He offers a sign in the future that will be granted only to those who already believe in him, namely his Resurrection.[3] There is an impasse. We say: "Give me a sign and I'll trust you." God says, "Trust me, and I'll give you a sign." Why can't we trust God first? This trust is required before we can have eyes to see and ears to hear the fullness of divine revelation in the scriptures.

Biblical Inspiration and Its Effects

What St. Paul said to the Thessalonians can be truly said of the whole of Scripture: "You received not a human word but, as it truly is, the word of God, that is now at work in you who believe" (1 Thess 2:13). The scriptures are the word of God because they are inspired by the Holy Spirit (2 Pet. 1:21). There is both a trinitarian and an incarnational aspect to the inspiration of Scripture. It is attributed to the Holy Spirit because it is the Holy Spirit's mission to reveal the Father through the Person of the Son. Therefore, "all Sacred Scripture is but one book, and the one book is Christ, because all divine Scripture speaks of Christ and is fulfilled in Christ."[4] And just as the Holy Spirit was the agent who formed the incarnate Word of God in the womb of the Virgin Mary, so too the Holy Spirit acts to form the word of God in the minds of the sacred authors so as to be kept in the heart of the Church.

Thus, the written word of God is likened to the incarnate Word: "Indeed the words of God, expressed in the words of men, are in every way like human language, just as the Word of the eternal Father, when he took on himself the flesh of human weakness, became like men" (*Dei Verbum* 13).

The Church has reflected more precisely on how inspiration takes place and on the relationship between the human authors and the divine author of Scripture. Since the written word of God is truly human and truly divine, it follows that God used the sacred authors as free and rational instruments, and so enlightened their minds that they first rightly understood and then put down in apt words everything and only what God wanted them to write (Leo XIII, *Providentissimus Deus*, II.D.3.a). Thus everything asserted by the sacred human author is asserted by the Holy Spirit (*Dei Verbum* 11).

As a consequence, the written word of God is free from error, so long as it is understood according to the intention of the sacred authors. The Holy Spirit is the Spirit of Truth, and therefore, the word inspired by him must be true. This freedom from error is one of the properties that follow from the divine inspiration of the Bible: "Just as the substantial Word of God became like men in every respect except sin, so too the words of God, expressed in human languages, became like human language in every respect except error" (Pius XII, *Divino Afflante Spiritu* 37).[5]

Yet the Spirit of Truth is also a Spirit of Love. This is another consequence of the trinitarian dimension of biblical inspiration. Just as the Word of God breathes forth a Spirit of Love, so too the written word of God must be understood as inspiring love in the hearts of those who understand it rightly. Thus, St. Augustine says in *On Christian Doctrine*: "Whoever, then, thinks that he understands the holy scriptures, or any part of them, but puts such an interpretation upon them as does not tend to build up this twofold love of God and our neighbor, does not yet understand them as he ought."[6] This is not to say that Sacred Scripture does not assert historical and philosophical truths. But when such truths are found asserted in Scripture, they have been put there for the purpose of promoting charity. The scriptures have been written for the sake of our salvation (*Dei Verbum* 11); hence, its truths are to be understood and interpreted in such a way that they promote charity.

There is another remarkable effect of biblical inspiration: the scriptures have both a *literal* sense and a *spiritual* sense. The literal sense is the sense directly intended and expressed by the words of the sacred author. The spiritual sense is the meaning of the things signified by the words of the literal sense.[7] Only a book inspired by God can have a spiritual sense, since God alone, as the lord of history, can make real, historical things and events clear signs of spiritual truths. The *Catechism of the Catholic Church* (CCC) explains the spiritual senses this way: "Thanks to the unity of God's plan, not only the text of Scripture, but also the realities and events about that it speaks can be signs" (117).

Let us take an example from the book of Exodus. In the story of the Exodus, the Israelites are in bondage to Pharaoh. But God sends Moses, who afflicts the Egyptians with ten plagues. The Israelites are allowed to flee, only to be pursued by the Egyptians to the shore of the Red Sea. But, led by an angel of the Lord, they pass through the Red Sea, into which the Egyptians are cast and drowned. They pass through the desert where they are fed by manna. But then they reach the border of the promised land and are too afraid to enter. So they are condemned to wander the desert for forty years until those who were afraid die off, and finally, they enter in and take possession of the promised land.

That's the literal account of the historical events of the Exodus. But these historical events can themselves be understood as signifying spiritual realities. The people of Israel can be understood as signifying an individual soul. Bondage to Pharaoh signifies bondage to the devil and sin. The ten plagues signify observance of the commandments of God, which serve to loosen the control of sin over the soul. The crossing of the Red Sea signifies passing through baptism, in which the forces of the devil are destroyed. The journey through the desert, led by the angel and fed with manna, signifies the journey of a soul through this life, fed by the Eucharist and led by its guardian angel. But if this soul reaches the border of heaven at death without being perfect, it must be purified in purgatory before it can enter. This corresponds to the forty years in the desert (the number forty signifies a time of cleansing and purgation). But once the time of purgation is over, the soul enters in and takes possession of the promised land at the resurrection of the body.[8]

The Fathers of the Church identified three distinct spiritual senses of Scripture: the moral sense, which teaches about how to act well; the allegorical, which teaches right belief about Christ and the Church in the present age; and the anagogical, which teaches right belief about Christ and the Church in the age to come (for example, the truths about death, judgment, heaven, and hell; see CCC 117).

Some Modern Obstacles to Reading the Word of God with Faith

In my experience teaching about the Bible, I have found that many people today find it difficult to place their faith in Scripture as the word of God. These difficulties are not without foundation. Many modern obstacles and challenges have been raised against the truth of Scripture. But in my experience, nearly all of them can be summarized under three headings:

1. The Bible contradicts modern science (for example, the creation account in Genesis seems to contradict what we now know about the origins of the universe from science);

2. The Bible contradicts itself (for example, there seem to be many inconsistencies among the four Gospel accounts); and

3. The authors of the Bible were biased (consciously or unconsciously) and therefore gave a doctored account that was not historically accurate.

I want to take up each of these three objections briefly (using three test cases) in order to lay out certain principles that can help overcome difficulties in approaching Scripture as the word of God.

1. "The Bible Contradicts Modern Science"

Let us take the creation account of the first chapter of Genesis as a test case for this objection.[9] The objection runs something like this: the Bible says that the world was made in seven days, and that God immediately created all the animals and plants. But we know from science that the universe is billions of years old and that the animals and plants on earth evolved over the course of millions of years. Therefore, the Bible teaches falsehood.

One of the most important things we need to do in order to understand Scripture is to read it carefully in order to see exactly what it intends to say. In the account of creation in Genesis, on which day was the sun created? The fourth day. From this one fact alone, we can deduce that the author of Genesis never intended for the seven days to mean seven twenty-four-hour time periods corresponding to rotations of the earth!

Well then, are the seven days of creation seven indefinite but chronological periods of time, as when St. Peter says that a thousand years are as a day in the sight of the Lord? This too is unlikely, since the plants were created before the sun, and even a simple farmer in Palestine knew that plants can't survive without sunlight. Besides, on the first day God divided light from darkness, and called light "day" and darkness "night." But then on fourth day he made the lights in the sky to divide the "day" and the "night." The first "day" and "night" cannot be the same as the second "day" and "night". So it seems unreasonable to interpret the seven days and nights of creation to refer to a strictly chronological order.

All this can be seen simply by reading the text closely, without any special exegetical knowledge. Treating the seven days of creation as seven twenty-four-hour periods is not reconcilable with the text itself: this is just one example of why it is important to read the Bible carefully and understand it on its own terms.

What is the message of the seven days of creation? Perhaps we can understand the creation account better if we look at the text again, keeping in mind the principle that the scriptures are written for the sake of our salvation and that our interpretation should promote right love of God and neighbor. In the first three days of creation the heavens, the sky (that holds the water) and the sea and dry land were formed. Then the next day the heavenly bodies (sun, moon, and stars) were created; then the next day, the animals were formed in the water; and finally, on the sixth day, animals and last of all man himself were formed out of the earth.

Looking back over that, we can see that water, earth, and sunlight are necessary for plants to live and flourish. Plants and luminous bodies (sun, moon, and stars) are necessary for animals to live and flourish. And finally, water, plants, luminous bodies, and animals are all necessary for man to live and flourish. The text is showing how things were ordained for the good of living things, especially animals and man. Also, we are beginning from heaven and descending to Earth. This seems to be because Moses, the traditional author of this account, especially wants to make clear to his people that the sun and moon and stars are *for man*, and so inferior to man, "lest perhaps lifting up your eyes to heaven, you see the sun and the moon, and all the stars of heaven, and being deceived by error you adore and serve them, that the Lord your God created for the service of all the nations that are under heaven" (Deut. 4:19). So we don't need to reconcile the first chapter of Genesis with a chronological order (that is the concern of science), since the order of concern here is a more profound and important order: *the order of intention of the Creator.* God wants to reveal to us something important for our salvation: what is made to serve what, and what is loved for the sake of what.

This approach to interpreting Scripture—reading the text carefully on its own terms and keeping in mind that it is revealing something important for our salvation—permits us to see that the conflict with the claims of modern science is not real, but only apparent. And a similar method can be used in other cases throughout the Bible.

2. "The Bible Contradicts Itself"

So much for the objection that the scriptures contradict modern science. But what about the more serious claim that the Bible contradicts itself? The number of apparently contradictory texts in Sacred Scripture is so great that it is impossible to take each one up one by one. However, it will suffice to give some principles and then apply them to a couple of test cases as a way of illustrating how apparent contradictions can be resolved.

The first principle is to *know what an actual contradiction looks like*. The second principle is to *read the text carefully*. The third principle is to *look at the original languages*, if necessary, and the possible meanings of each term. To illustrate, I will apply these three principles to two texts in which an apparent contradiction exists.

One text of the Gospel often cited as a contradiction is the account of the temptation of Christ in the desert. This event is recorded in the Gospels of Matthew and Luke (Matt. 4:1–11 and Luke 4:1–13), yet with a significant difference: the passage in Matthew gives a different order of temptations than Luke does. In Matthew's Gospel, the order is (1) the temptation to turn stones into bread; (2) the temptation to cast himself from the pinnacle of the temple; and (3) the temptation to be made a king. In Luke, the order is: (1) the temptation to turn stones into bread; (2) the temptation to be made a king; and (3) the temptation to cast himself from the pinnacle of the temple. The second and third temptations are switched.

Now obviously, they cannot have happened in both ways. It seems that one has to be right and the other wrong. To resolve this apparent contradiction, we first need to read the text carefully. We see that Luke has a small change in relation to Matthew, only a single word in fact: a simple connecting word between the temptations. But this word makes all the difference. Matthew gives the account of Jesus being tempted to change stones into bread and connects this with the next temptation about the temple with the word *then* (*tote* in Greek): "Then the devil took him," etc. But Luke gives the account of Jesus being tempted to change stones into bread and connects this with the next temptation about being made king with the word *and* (*kai* in Greek): "And [the devil] brought him," etc.

What Is the Significance of This Change?

If you were to ask me what I did today and I responded by telling you, "I went to the store, *then* I went to the bank, *then* I went to a movie," and later on someone else were to ask me the same question and I responded by saying, "I went to the store *and* I went to a movie *and* I went to the bank," would I have necessarily contradicted myself? No, for the word *then* implies a chronological order but the word *and* does not. So there is no contradiction between Luke's account and Matthew's account. Indeed, we can suppose that Luke changed that one little word in order to preserve the truth of his account despite presenting a slightly different order.

Which raises the larger question here, namely: Why would Luke change the order? That opens up another important principle for reading the Gospels. Each evangelist had a particular theological aim, and so each arranged the material in his Gospel to best accomplish this aim. For example, the Fathers of the Church noticed that Matthew's Gospel focused on the mysteries of the Incarnation of Christ, and his kingship, whereas Luke's Gospel focused on the mysteries of Christ's Passion and his priesthood. This could explain why Luke would place the temptation for Christ to cast himself from the pinnacle of the temple last, since it seems to have been a temptation to make himself the high priest (see Hebrews 5:5). And Luke was primarily interested in Christ's priesthood.

Another consequence of the differing theological aims of the evangelists is their omission of significant facts that others record in order to make their theological insights stand out better in relief. This is why, for example, all sorts of significant events are omitted by the different evangelists in the varying Resurrection accounts (for example, Matthew mentions an angel rolling away the stone, whereas the others omit this very significant event).

As a teacher, I understand this method very well. If I am teaching physics and want to explain the law of the acceleration of falling bodies, I may intentionally omit all sorts of real-life facts in order to isolate the different principles at work. For example, I will make no reference to friction or viscosity of the air, I will not mention the effects of wind or the shape of the falling body, I won't talk about how far the body is from the center of the Earth, etc. To add in all these significant real-life factors would serve only to confuse and overwhelm the student, so I talk only about the law that a body increases in velocity in proportion to the time that it is falling.

That's only part of the story, but it is a true part. And by telling that part, I can teach the student more effectively about that one principle responsible for the motion of falling bodies. Later on, I can talk about those other factors in isolation, and once everything has been treated separately, we can combine all the principles to see what happens in real life.

Something like that happens in the Gospels. St. John tells us that if everything Jesus did and said were written down, the whole world could not contain the books that would be written (John 21:25). In other words, the student would be overwhelmed! So each of the evangelists highlighted or even isolated certain mysteries of Christ's life so they would stand out in relief: John focuses upon Christ's divinity, the others on mysteries of his humanity (such as his kingship, priesthood, and role as prophet). Therefore, each evangelist omits certain significant events that the others record, and all the Gospels put together form a more complete account of what happened in the life of Jesus. So the differences in, for example, the varying Resurrection accounts are not really contradictions. They are each part of the whole story. St. Augustine beautifully reconstructs this more complete whole in his work *The Harmony of the Gospels.*

I mentioned above that sometimes it may be necessary to employ another helpful principle in resolving apparent contradictions in the Bible: looking at its original languages. One example where this solves an apparent contradiction involves the chapters of Ezekiel 26 and Isaiah 23. Ezekiel 26:21 seems to assert that the city of Tyre will never be rebuilt again, whereas Isaiah 23:17 seems to say that Tyre will be rebuilt after seventy years. This appears to be a contradiction.

But the Hebrew word used in Ezekiel 26:21 is *od*, which has a double meaning: it can mean "forever" but it can also signify "until the jubilee," when everything is restored (after fifty years). For example, it is used in this second sense in Exodus 21:6. If here *od* is translated in this second sense, then the apparent contradiction between Isaiah 23 and Ezekiel 26 disappears.

These two test cases illustrate the principles that can be used to overcome objections that the Bible contradicts itself. The same principles can be applied in similar cases where there appears to be a contradiction.

3. "The Authors of the Bible Were Biased"

One final obstacle to faith in the word of God that modern readers often encounter is the claim that the authors of Scripture (especially the authors of the Gospels) were biased and therefore did not give truthful accounts of what happened. Rather, the objection runs, their accounts are doctored to include fictional elements for the sake of persuading readers to accept their religious positions. In short, the objection asserts that the evangelists were actually propagandists, not truthful transmitters of divine revelation.

Of course, this was a claim being made even in the time of the apostles. Peter expressly rejects this objection in his second epistle: "We did not follow cleverly devised myths when we made known to you the power and coming of our Lord Jesus Christ, but we had been eyewitnesses of his majesty" (2 Pet. 1:16). And the veracity of their accounts was something each of them defended even to the shedding of their blood. It is hard to believe that so many people would be willing to give their lives for the sake of a lie.

But there is perhaps an even more powerful response to this objection than the witness of the apostles' martyrdoms, found in the simple fact that the Gospels contain all sorts of embarrassing passages that cannot be reconciled with the position that the evangelists were writing propaganda.

For example, many of the accounts of the Resurrection state that the disciples did not at first recognize Jesus. Even the final Resurrection account of Matthew's Gospel states that "some doubted" after seeing Jesus. Moreover, the evangelists note that the first witnesses of the Resurrection were women, even though, in that time and culture, women were not regarded as reliable witnesses and were even excluded from being witnesses in legal trials. The Gospels also include several accounts of the moral failings of the apostles. If the evangelists were attempting to write propaganda, they would never have included passages like these, since they might have caused their readers to doubt. Propaganda would have included only the strongest evidence, put forth by morally unassailable witnesses. But the evangelists were not propagandists, and these passages found their way into the Gospels because they are true. They accurately reflect what happened.

So, with the trustworthiness of the scriptures—and the Gospels in particular—in mind, let us proceed to some tools that will help us reflect upon the conversations and parables of Jesus.

CHAPTER 2

TOOLS FOR DIGGING

St. Thomas Aquinas once made an interesting observation: whereas nature equips other animals with all the tools they need for acquiring the goods that perfect them (like claws and sharp teeth for fighting, or a hard shell for protection), human beings need to use their minds to make tools. The same is true about understanding Scripture: we don't naturally understand everything in Scripture. We need to use our minds to find tools to dig more deeply into the hidden truths and meanings of Scripture.

Let's begin with a simple principle: there are no useless or unimportant words in Sacred Scripture. Every word in Scripture has a purpose and a meaning. Jesus once said that we would be judged for every idle word (Matt. 12:36). Certainly, the word of God will not have idle words! Thomas goes so far as to say that every word of Scripture is a participation in the eternal Word of God: "For Christ is naturally the Word of God; moreover, every word inspired by God is a certain participated likeness of him."[10] Since this is true, we should notice every detail and seek to understand distinctly the meaning of every word as we read through the scriptures. The Spirit is in the details! With this in mind, here are some tools you can use to dig more deeply into God's word.

Tool #1: Definition

Since every word of Scripture has a profound meaning, it is always helpful to try and understand each word more distinctly. Definition is a tool for doing just that. For example, what does it mean when Jesus says that some seed fell on "the path"? By defining the word "path" we can get a better idea. A path is a hardened surface formed on the ground where people often walk. Moreover, a path is not itself a destination, but is always a means to some other destination. This more distinct understanding allows us to understand the kind of persons Jesus is talking about when he says they are like a path. These are people whose hearts are hardened because others have used them as mere means.

Tool #2: Coincidences

Very often in the scriptures, you will notice what seem to be coincidences. But just as there are no mere coincidences in God's providential care for us, since "all things work for good for those who love God" (Rom. 8:28), so also, there are no mere coincidences in Scripture. Take the example of Luke, chapter eight, verses 42–43: "[Jairus] had an only daughter, almost twelve years old, and she was dying. And it happened as he went, that he was thronged by the multitudes. And there was a certain woman having an issue of blood twelve years." It seems to be a coincidence that the woman has had a hemorrhage for the entire lifetime of Jairus's daughter. But in fact, this becomes a clue to a deeper understanding of the passage; namely, the analogy between the way we treat others and the way God treats us (see chapter nine for more details).

Tool #3: Three or More Parallels

Parallels are abundant in all written works; many of them are generic and simply result from there being recurring patterns in human experience. But when multiple parallels are found in two passages, this points to something intended by the author to draw our attention. The same is true in Scripture. In my experience, whenever two passages of Scripture have three or more parallels, it points to an important hidden truth that needs to be investigated.

Take the example of the parallels between the life of the Blessed Virgin Mary and Zachary, the father of John the Baptist. There is an annunciation to Zachary followed by an annunciation to Mary (both by Gabriel). Both Zachary and Mary ask a question. Both receive an answer that includes a sign about Elizabeth conceiving. Both go to Zachary's house to Elizabeth. Both end with a canticle of praise of God. Those are five parallels. So it is obvious that St. Luke wants us to compare Mary and Zachary. There are obvious similarities, but also significant differences. Zachary's question is one of doubt, Mary's question, although superficially like Zachary's is actually a question prompted by faith. She asks not whether the angel's word will be accomplished, but how. Zachary's sign is a punishment to help bring about faith, Mary's sign is a reward for faith. This leads us to the event of the Visitation.

St. Luke tells us that Zachary "went to his home" and "after these days his wife Elizabeth conceived, and for five months she hid herself" (Luke 1:23–24, RSV). When Zachary comes to Elizabeth, he conceives John in a carnal way, by earthly means. But when Mary comes to Elizabeth, what happens? At Mary's word, Elizabeth is "filled with the Holy Spirit" and the infant John "leaped for joy." This seems to be the fulfillment of the word of the angel concerning John: "He will be filled with the Holy Spirit, even from his mother's womb" (Luke 1:15, RSV). The analogy between Zachary and Mary is striking: when Mary speaks, Elizabeth and John are filled with the Holy Spirit, with a divine life. Just as Zachary is an instrument in causing natural life, Mary is an instrument in causing supernatural life. In other words, Mary is revealed to be a mediatrix of grace; that is, of divine life in souls. And if Mary's word is somehow instrumental in the grace given to Elizabeth and John at the Visitation, it is not difficult to look back at Mary's word at the moment of the Incarnation to see how Mary becomes even an instrument to bring about the grace of the Incarnation itself. God made the Incarnation, the source of all other graces, depend upon Mary's word of consent.

Tool #4: Strange or Unique Facts

Sometimes Scripture records strange or unique facts—that is, facts that seem out of place or occur only once. Often these are openings to some deeper insight. John, chapter nine, records one such strange fact: "Never since the world began has it been heard that anyone opened the eyes of a man born blind" (John 9:32, RSV). Why is that? Certainly greater miracles than healing a man born blind had been done (for example, Elisha the prophet raised someone from the dead). Yet, there is a special spiritual significance of blindness from birth: it signifies a kind of sin from birth. And this opens up the meaning of the passage in which Jesus heals the man born blind (see chapter seven for more details).

An example of a singular or unique event in Scripture is the passage about Jesus and the woman with a hemorrhage in Luke, chapter eight. There Jesus calls her his daughter. This is the only time in Scripture when Jesus calls someone his daughter. We are meant to ponder this unique fact. Among other things, it points to the analogy between Jesus and Jairus: both of them have a daughter who is in need of healing. This sheds light on the entire encounter between Jesus and Jairus (see chapter nine for more details).

Tool #5: Things You Expect to Be Said That Are Left Unsaid

Human beings love patterns because they are predictable, and you know what to expect with a pattern. But sometimes the pattern doesn't go as we expect, and it leaves us with a sense of wonder or surprise. This happens very often in Scripture, and it is an indication of another place to start digging. Jesus' parables, especially, leave things unsaid when you expect them to be said.

Take the parable of the servants with the talents from Matthew chapter twenty-five. There we hear about three servants who each receive a different number of talents from their master and are commanded to trade with them until he returns. Two of them do just that, and they succeed at doubling their talents; but the third refuses to trade. The reason he gives is that it is risky and he might lose the talent he was given. That immediately raises a question: why doesn't the parable give an example of someone who trades and fails: someone who loses his talents or at least loses some of them? One possible answer is that, although it is a logical possibility, it is not a real possibility for those who obey God, the master. This underscores the great generosity of God toward his servants, since God assures success to all who obey him.

Tool #6: Learn Some Greek or Hebrew

This tool may not be for everyone, but you would be surprised at how just a little effort, using a dictionary, can still provide many benefits. Official translations are usually done by experts and should be considered trustworthy; nevertheless, no translation can ever capture the variety of meanings a Greek or Hebrew word might have. The translator always has to pick a single word or phrase to translate the original text, and that word or phrase will almost never be an exact equivalent. Besides this, sometimes the same Greek or

Hebrew word will have to be translated using two different English words, so that the reader of the translation is not aware that the same word was used in the original. Some Bibles are published with the translations between the lines of the original (called an interlinear text). These can be especially helpful in getting a more exact understanding of what is being said.

For example, in John chapter eight, when Jesus is with the woman caught in adultery, it twice records that Jesus bent down and began to "write" on the ground. Nearly all English translations use the same word, "write," to translate two distinct Greek words: *kategraphen*—that is used the first time Jesus bends down; and *egraphen*—that is used the second time Jesus bends down. The first of these Greek words, which is probably better translated as "engrave" rather than "write," appears only once in the New Testament, but it is found in the Septuagint text of the Old Testament. There it almost always refers to a single event: the engraving of the commandments on the tablets of stone by the finger of God. That obviously sheds a whole new light on the passage (see chapter four for more details).

So those are some tools that anyone can use to dig more deeply into the scriptures. Now it's time to put some of those tools to use in some parables and conversations of Jesus. But before we do that, one more thing needs to be said: nothing can replace prayer and an open heart as ways to come to understand the scriptures more deeply. Understanding Scripture is not just a matter of applying techniques. It always involves establishing a relationship with the Author of Scripture. The words of a stranger and the words of someone whose heart we know well do not bear the same content. We are much more likely to understand the nuances of the person whose heart we know well.

So we need to have a deep relationship with the Holy Spirit by means of the gifts of the Holy Spirit, especially the gift of understanding, if we are to fully profit from using these tools. It is this disposition of heart that forms the subject of our first parable.

CHAPTER 3

PARABLES ABOUT SOWERS AND SEEDS

Before entering into an explanation of these parables, perhaps a word ought to be said about what a parable is and why it needs explanation in the first place. A parable is a verbal expression, usually a story, whether spoken or written, that uses figures and images to communicate profound truths. Precisely because the truths that are communicated are profound, attempts to express them in plain language to ordinary people can be difficult. In some way, a parable proportions these profound truths to ordinary people, but paradoxically leaves many things hidden at the same time: a parable simultaneously reveals and hides truth. St. Thomas explains this paradox in the first question of his *Summa Theologiae*:

> God provides for all things in a way befitting to their natures. But it is natural for man to come to understandable things by way of sensible things, since all our knowledge has its beginning from sense. It follows that spiritual things are fittingly handed on to us under bodily metaphors.

As Dionysius says, "It is impossible for the divine ray to shine upon us unless it be covered over by a variety of sacred veils." It is also fitting that Sacred Scripture propose spiritual realities under bodily likenesses, since Scripture is commonly proposed to all . . . so that the unlearned might grasp at least a little, since they are not disposed to grasp the intelligible things in themselves.[11]

In other words, the parable serves the purpose of giving spiritual nourishment to the simple and unlearned while allowing for even more profound nourishment for those who seek to understand its deeper truths through prayer and study. In fact, a parable is often deliberately open-ended, or sometimes even unconcluded, to stimulate reflection in the hearer so that he will internalize its meaning by reflection. Therefore, it can be very beneficial to meditate on and investigate deeper the hidden truths found in these parables of our Lord.

The Parable About the Sower
Who Sows the Seed of the Word

In Mark, Jesus tells a parable about the sower who went out to sow the word of God. I have chosen to begin with this parable because it is one that has already been explained by Jesus. And so, by imitating his method of exposition, we can start to understand each of the parables with Jesus' help. There is a second reason I have decided to begin with this parable. It is that Jesus himself indicates that it seems to contain the key for unlocking all the parables when he says, "Do you not understand this parable? Then how will you understand any of the parables?" So by understanding this parable, we will be more able to understand the other parables of Jesus. Here is the text:

On another occasion he began to teach by the sea. A very large crowd gathered around him so that he got into a boat on the sea and sat down. And the whole crowd was beside the sea on land. And he taught them at length in parables, and in the course of his instruction he said to them, "Hear this! A sower went out to sow. And as he sowed, some seed fell on the path, and the birds came and ate it up. Other seed fell on rocky ground where it had little soil. It sprang up at once because the soil was not deep. And when the sun rose, it was scorched and it withered for lack of roots. Some seed fell among thorns, and the thorns grew up and choked it and it produced no grain. And some seed fell on rich soil and produced fruit. It came up and grew and yielded thirty, sixty, and a hundredfold." He added, "Whoever has ears to hear ought to hear."

And when he was alone, those present along with the Twelve questioned him about the parables. He answered them, "The mystery of the kingdom of God has been granted to you. But to those outside everything comes in parables, so that 'they may look and see but not perceive, and hear and listen but not understand, in order that they may not be converted and be forgiven.'" Jesus said to them, "Do you not understand this parable? Then how will you understand any of the parables? The sower sows the word. These are the ones on the path where the word is sown. As soon as they hear, Satan comes at once and takes away the word sown in them. And these are the ones sown on rocky ground who, when they hear the word, receive it at once with joy. But they have no root; they last only for a time. Then when tribulation or persecution comes because of the word, they quickly fall away. Those sown among thorns are another sort. They are the people who hear the word, but worldly anxiety, the lure of riches, and the craving for other things intrude and choke the word, and it bears no fruit. But those sown on rich soil are the ones who hear the word and accept it and bear fruit thirty and sixty and a hundredfold" (Mark 4:1–20).

Let us begin by asking why Jesus says, *If you do not understand this parable, how will you understand all the parables?* Is it because this one is easier to understand than all the others (since the metaphors are clearer)? This does not seem likely, since many parables seem to use simpler metaphors. Is it because the principles of interpretation of this parable are presupposed for the others? This seems unlikely too. For Jesus does not say "if you do not understand the principles of interpretation of this parable, how will you understand any of the parables?" Besides, other parables seem to use the same principles, so why would this parable be special?

The reason why understanding this parable is necessary for understanding the other parables seems to be that the truths revealed in this parable are somehow presupposed to understanding the truths revealed in all the other parables. For this parable is about receiving (that is, hearing and understanding) the word of God. And of course, all the parables are included among the word of God. Jesus is saying that unless one clears his soul of the hard ground and the stones and weeds that this parable signifies, he will not be able to understand any parable, or any teaching of Christ. Moreover, Jesus also instructs them that they are not capable of understanding any of the parables without his help.

This is the first step each of us must take: we must not be a hard path, nor rocky, shallow soil, nor soil mixed with thorns, if we are to understand the conversations and parables of Jesus. We should try to understand better what each of these impediments to the word of God signifies. And to do this, we need to look at the parable again more carefully.

The Context of the Parable

Each of Jesus' parables has a context. St. Mark begins by explaining that Jesus *began to teach by the sea. A very large crowd gathered around him so that he got into a boat on the sea and sat down. And the whole crowd was beside the sea on land. And he taught them at length in parables.* Every detail in the word of God has meaning. God does not use idle words. So it is significant that Jesus teaches while sitting in a boat on the sea, while the large crowd was beside the sea on the land. The land is a place of security and stability, whereas the sea is a place of insecurity and flux. A boat is a vessel used to cross the sea, to get from land on one side to land on the other. At the beginning of his teaching, the people wanted to cling to their own certainties: they wanted to judge reality by their own minds. The idea of accepting a revelation from God that was beyond their comprehension was a fearful prospect, since they could no longer be the ultimate judge of what is true and good. This is what is signified by the crowd standing on the land. And there is a legitimate desire they are trying to fulfill by standing on something certain and fixed. But Jesus knows that this desire for a perfect and firm grasp of truth, goodness, and reality is something they can have only on the other side of the sea—in our heavenly homeland.

Therefore, Jesus gets into a boat, symbolizing the Church, on the sea, symbolizing the insecurity of faith. Jesus is trying to coax them by his example to "go out into the deep" beyond their own knowledge and judgments. For "eye has not seen, nor has ear heard, nor has it entered into the heart of man, the good things that God has prepared for those who love him" (1 Cor. 2:9). So long as we are willing to accept as true and good only the things we ourselves can judge by our own minds, we are condemned to a "salvation" that is no better and no bigger than ourselves. This risk of faith is necessary if the soul is to cross over into that truly firm and stable land of the vision of God. If we are to pass from standing on our own power to standing on God's power, we must cross the sea of faith. And so the context of this parable about receiving the word of God is fitting, since it manifests the need for faith and trust.

Reading Between the Lines of the Parables: What Jesus Doesn't Say

There is another significant principle we should follow in reading the parables of Jesus: namely, we should attend not only to what Jesus says, but what he doesn't say. Remember, parables are often left open or unconcluded for the sake of stimulating reflection. Although Jesus explains the parable in part, he does not explain every detail or aspect of the parable. He wants you to ask questions about the parts he does not explain. For example, in this parable Jesus does not explain why the sower scattered seed on bad soil; nor does he explain the significance of the thirty, sixty, or hundredfold. He wants us to spend time in prayer and meditation seeking out the deeper meaning left unsaid. Even Jesus' silence speaks. And sometimes the passages he does not explain are as important as those he explains.

First, it is important to notice that Jesus compares the word of God to a seed. A seed is the beginning of a living thing, and it has the remarkable ability to transform non-living matter like earth and water into something living. So too, the word of God is the beginning of the divine life within us. And compared to that divine life, our human nature and our human life is like nonliving matter, like bare earth. The word of God draws each part of our human life into itself and transforms our human life into a truly divine life. But this transformation is something gradual and continuous. It does not happen all at once, any more than a tree sprouts up all at once. Therefore, in coming to the scriptures, we need to be patient, not thinking that we will be able to understand everything in the beginning, nor thinking that we will be able to live according to the demands of the word of God perfectly from the beginning.

It is interesting that the sower scatters the seed indiscriminately—over paths and rocky ground as well as over good soil. It is easy to understand why a human sower would do this, because he cannot control where every seed lands. But the divine sower seems to be able to choose, so why would Jesus, who said that we should not cast our "pearls before swine" (Matt. 7:6). scatter the seed of his word onto unworthy and indisposed recipients? Because God desires that all should be saved, and so he offers the gift of salvation to all, even those whom he knows will reject it. He refuses to let our wickedness and hardness of heart be a limit to his goodness and mercy. And so this gesture of scattering the seed everywhere signifies the mercy of God toward all men. If we are not transformed by the seed of the word, it is not because God never offered. The inability to enter into the divine life is due to our own freely chosen defects, not God's stinginess. Therefore, we should consider more carefully what each of these defects means and how we might be free from them.

The Path

A path is formed along the ground where people often walk. Moreover, a path is not a destination, but a means to some other destination. As a result, the ground becomes so hard that nothing can penetrate. Seeds thrown on the path remain there, never entering into the earth, never transforming it. And eventually, the birds come, and the seed never even starts to grow. Just as the ground where people often walk grows hard, so too the heart that is trampled upon and used by others, a heart that allows others to use it as a mere means rather than to love it as an end, a "destination," grows hard. St. Paul accuses some of the Corinthians of acting in this way: "For you put up with it if someone enslaves you, or devours you, or gets the better of you, or puts on airs, or slaps you in the face" (2 Cor. 11:20). The heart ceases to believe it can be loved, and so it falls deaf to the appeal of the Father's love. The word *never* enters into such a heart, and eventually, the demons come and convince such a person that there is no point in even listening anymore to such words. The word is then taken away from them before it even gets a chance to take root and transform them. If we are to be transformed from a path into fertile soil, we must stop allowing ourselves to be used by others. We must recognize our dignity as made in the image of God, as someone made for happiness and love.

The Rocky, Shallow Soil

Unlike a path, rocky soil is not completely hardened. It has areas that are soft enough to take in the seed. But this soil is shallow and there is not room for growth, so although it seems to spring up right away, the growth of the seed is stunted. When the heat of the sun beats down upon such a plant, it does not have sufficient roots to draw water and nourishment from the soil to stay alive, and so it is scorched, withers, and dies.

Similar to this kind of soil are those people who seem on the surface to have genuine openness to God's word and his love. But this is only a veneer, a façade. At a deeper level, their hearts are still hardened by their sinful attachments and fears. They live by their emotions and follow what is pleasing for the moment, and so when they hear the Gospel, together with its promise of eternal life, they at first welcome this message as something pleasing, *with joy*. The word begins to grow and develop, and transform whatever soil is there into a living being. Their conversion seems sincere and is often accompanied by an initial zeal and enthusiasm. But soon enough the word encounters the parts of the mind or the heart that are closed off to conversion.

For example, there may be truths revealed by God that seem contrary to what we want to hold. We are so used to our customary ways of thinking that we cannot give up these human doctrines for the sake of receiving divine doctrines. We do not allow every thought to be taken "captive in obedience to Christ" (2 Cor. 10:5).[12] There are also rocks in our hearts: those darker, hidden parts of the heart that the soul does not want to give over to God to be transformed and vivified. These rocks can be our habitual or customary ways of thinking, those fashionable ideas of the world that are incompatible with the teaching of Jesus. They can also be moral dispositions that we consider "non-negotiable." There is a sinful relationship we cannot give up for the sake of the Gospel, or an attachment to some creature we deem necessary for happiness. When push comes to shove, these ideas and moral dispositions harden and do not allow the word of God to enter in and transform those parts of our life. Consequently, the word no longer seems pleasing when the demands of conversion are placed on it. And as soon as there is a price to pay for keeping the word, either through persecutions, ridicule, or interior or exterior trials, the life that has begun to grow in that soul does not have sufficient resources of grace, the water of the soul, to survive these painful experiences. And so the life of God diminishes and eventually dies.

If we are to be transformed from rocky, shallow soil into fertile soil, we must permit God to enter every part of our hearts. There must be no aspect of our lives or of our being that is non-negotiable or off-limits to God. And this requires docility, humility, and contrition. In fact, the word "contrition" means to crush or break apart. Contrition crushes the rocks in our hearts and turns them into soil.

The Thorny Soil

Those souls who correspond to the thorny soil are quite different from those whose hearts are like rocky soil. These souls do not harden their hearts and refuse to let God enter. And their conversion is more sincere and lasting, so the roots grow more deeply. The problem with these souls is not that they refuse to let God in, but rather that they permit thorns to enter in as well. These thorns are the desires for riches, worldly gain, and in general the desire to find happiness in this life. Such souls say to themselves: "Yes, I want to be happy in the life to come, so I will follow the Gospel; but I also want to be happy in this life, and so I will seek an abundance of this world's goods too."

The problem with this thinking is that love for the world is incompatible with love for God. Jesus says simply: "Whoever loves his life loses it, and whoever hates his life in this world will preserve it for eternal life" (John 12:25). And St. John says, "Do not love the world or the things of the world. If anyone loves the world, the love of the Father is not in him" (1 John 2:15). The love for the things of this world is aptly described by weeds, since the love for the things of this world makes the dead soil of our hearts feel alive, at least for a short time. But these weeds are only mimicking the wheat. They are hard to tell apart when they are young, but soon enough the weeds turn ugly and deform our hearts. The soil of our hearts will either be transformed into a divine life by the seed of the word, or it will be transformed into a demonic life by the seed of the evil one. The two cannot exist side by side, and if we insist on holding onto our desire for earthly happiness, the life of God in us will eventually be choked off.

In the Sermon on the Mount, the Lord warns us against a tendency that he knew would surface in the hearts of his disciples: the tendency to hedge our bets and try to be happy both in this life and in the next; to accept the bare minimum of suffering necessary for salvation, and in the meantime try to enjoy as much happiness as one can in this present life. But the so-called "happiness" of this life is transitory and illusory, whereas the happiness promised by the Lord in the Beatitudes is real and eternal. In fact, they are even contrary to one another: to the extent we seek for the one, we exclude the other. Our Lady once said to Bernadette of Lourdes: "I do not promise you happiness in this life, but only in the life to come."[13]

Someone might object: So are we to live this life constantly in mourning and dejection? What about the Scripture passages that tell us to "rejoice always" (1 Thess. 5:16; Phil. 4:4)? It is true that we are always to rejoice, but to rejoice in the Lord, not in the world. We are called to have joy in the Lord while we pass through this life, but we are not to find happiness here. God does not want to have to drag us kicking and screaming into heaven because we like it here so much!

How can we avoid being thorny soil? By placing all our hope in the goods of the life to come, and none of our hope in this life. And although this may seem difficult, the grace of Christ makes it easier than it seems. A simple comparison will help illustrate. Imagine that you have a dear friend: someone whom you love as your own self. When you are together, you are always happy, and when you are apart you are sad. And it happens that the Lord gives you a choice. On the one hand, you can be constantly together with your friend for some weeks or months or even years, but after that time you will forever be separated from your friend. Or, on the other hand, you can be apart from your friend for some weeks or months or even years, but after that time you will always and forever be together with your friend.

Which of the two would you choose? It is obvious that you would choose the second. Why? Because if you chose the first, even the time you were together with your friend would be seasoned with bitterness because of the impending and inevitable separation. You couldn't even enjoy the time you were together. But if you chose the second, even the time you were apart from your friend would be seasoned with joy because of your anticipation of the inevitable, permanent reunion. In fact, our present joy on account of our hope for future goods will be greater than the joy we would have had in the actual possession of temporal goods. The hopeful Christian is more joyful in this life than the man who possesses all the goods of this world. Not only that, but the longer we live the greater our joy becomes. We should be marking off the days of the calendar, with our joy increasing after every passing day. This is how the Christian soul should be: our joy increasing with every passing day that we come closer to eternity. I remember once as a teenager coming across a poem that an elderly nun used to recite as she did her knitting. It went like this:

One day more of work for Jesus
One day less of life for me.
But heaven is nearer
And Christ is dearer
Than yesterday to me.

That very beautifully expresses the sentiments of the Christian heart. If we choose to put our hopes and find our joy in the passing things of this world, then we will inevitably find disappointment. We will be like those who chose the first option: to be with the one we love only for a short time, only to be separated from him forever. But if we place all our hope in the life to come, in Christ, then we are like those who chose the second option: to be separated from the one we love for a short time, only to be reunited with him forever.

The Produce of the Good Soil:
Thirty, Sixty, and a Hundredfold

Finally, we do well to ask about the produce of the good soil. What does Jesus intend to signify by the varying numbers of produce produced by the heart that hears and accepts the word of God? First, the fact that the grain that dies produces more like itself is instructive. The hearts that hear and accept the seed of the word produces other seeds, and therefore the implication is that they too share in the labor of the sower. They spread the word of God to others so that it may grow in their hearts too. This is what happened to the Samaritan woman at the well: "Many of the Samaritans of that town began to believe in him because of the word of the woman" (John 4:39). Second, the diverse numbers of grain signify that God bestows his gifts freely—more on some, less on others, according to his wisdom: "But one and the same Spirit produces all of these, distributing them individually to each person as he wishes" (1 Cor. 12:11). This should not be source of envy, but of joy, since we are all members of the same body, and the gifts of each are shared by all.

Finally, it is fruitful to meditate upon the specific numbers indicated by the Lord. The number thirty is the multiplication of three and ten. Faith in the Trinity is signified by the number three; observance of the Ten Commandments is signified by the number ten. So the thirtyfold signifies one who has faith and keeps the commandments. But the number sixty is double thirty. And this signifies one who follows a double law: both the commandments and the evangelical counsels: "If you wish to be perfect, go, sell what you have and give to the poor, and you will have treasure in heaven. Then come, follow me" (Matt. 19:21). But the number 100 signifies completeness or perfection in the scriptures. Thus, the flock of the Lord is said to have a hundred sheep (Matt. 18:12; Luke 15:4). And the most complete and perfect love of all is shown by the martyrs: "No one has greater love than this, to lay down one's life for one's friends" (John 15:13).

Thus, the three degrees of fruit can be referred to the faithful lay folk (thirty), the religious who follow the evangelical counsels (sixty), and the martyrs (a hundred). This corresponds to how Thomas Aquinas understood this text.[14]

By considering how great is the reward for those who hear the word of God and cherish it in their hearts, we are moved to greater zeal to prepare our hearts to receive the seed of the word. We can see better now why understanding this parable is somehow presupposed as a preparation for understanding all the other parables.

The Parable About the Wheat and the Weeds

In Matthew, Jesus tells another parable about a sower who sows seed, but this time he adds another dimension to the parable. He speaks also about the growing up of weeds together with the wheat. He explains the origin of the weeds and the reason they are allowed to remain, as well as their ultimate destiny.

He proposed another parable to them. "The kingdom of heaven may be likened to a man who sowed good seed in his field. While everyone was asleep his enemy came and sowed weeds all through the wheat, and then went off. When the crop grew and bore fruit, the weeds appeared as well. The slaves of the householder came to him and said, 'Master, did you not sow good seed in your field? Where have the weeds come from?' He answered, 'An enemy has done this.' His slaves said to him, 'Do you want us to go and pull them up?' He replied, 'No, if you pull up the weeds you might uproot the wheat along with them. Let them grow together until harvest; then at harvest time I will say to the harvesters, "First collect the weeds and tie them in bundles for burning; but gather the wheat into my barn."'. . . Then, dismissing the crowds, he went into the house. His disciples approached him and said, "Explain to us the parable of the weeds in the field."

He said in reply, "He who sows good seed is the Son of Man, the field is the world, the good seed the children of the kingdom. The weeds are the children of the evil one, and the enemy who sows them is the devil. The harvest is the end of the age, and the harvesters are angels. Just as weeds are collected and burned [up] with fire, so will it be at the end of the age. The Son of Man will send his angels, and they will collect out of his kingdom all who cause others to sin and all evildoers. They will throw them into the fiery furnace, where there will be wailing and grinding of teeth. Then the righteous will shine like the sun in the kingdom of their Father. Whoever has ears ought to hear (Matt. 13:24–33, 36–40).

At first, this seems as if it is a more detailed explanation of the souls who allow thorns to grow in the soil of their hearts. But a careful reading shows that the field here is not an individual soul, but the whole world, and each stalk of wheat and each weed corresponds to an individual person, not just to the desires in a person's heart. The parable is addressing a perennial problem faced by the children of the kingdom: Why does God permit so much evil in the world, and even in the Church? This seems especially true under the New Covenant. Under the Old Covenant, often enough the wicked would be slain by an act of God: fire from heaven, the earth swallowing them up, a plague, and so on. And when we see so much evil done in the world, and so little retribution from God, the believer can become frustrated, longing for the good old days of the Old Covenant, when sinners were on the run. But this parable is an antidote for such thoughts. God's ways are not our ways, and endurance of evil during this life is part and parcel of the new dispensation. So that is the overall message of this parable: why God permits evil people to flourish. As with the previous parable, Jesus himself gives an explanation; and, as with the previous parable, in his explanation he is silent about the meaning of some important parts of this parable.

I want to focus only on one unexplained text of this parable: namely, the part where, in response to the slaves' offer to pull up the weeds, he replies: *No, if you pull up the weeds you might uproot the wheat along with them. Let them grow together until harvest.* Jesus is completely silent about the meaning of this part of the parable, and yet it is clearly mysterious given his interpretation of the other parts that surround it. If the harvesters are the angels, and the wheat are the just and the weeds are the wicked, then what could it mean to say that the wheat might be uprooted with the weeds? Is there some danger that the angels might mistakenly snatch up a good person and throw him into hell? That doesn't seem likely, and it's bad theology. What could this passage mean?

One possibility is that when evil men are allowed to oppress and persecute the just, this is the occasion for the just to grow in certain virtues: patience, charity, forgiveness, even martyrdom. And unless they had been given these opportunities, the just would not have grown as strong as they did. If God immediately struck down every wicked person, there would be a scarcity of people to forgive, and few opportunities to persevere through persecution. The Church would be bereft of martyrs. In effect, by taking away the wicked (the weeds), the just (the wheat) would not be able to grow to full maturity. And there is much to be said for this interpretation.

But I want to propose another possible reading, one that I think is more in keeping with the text and the intention of our Lord. Unlike natural wheat and weeds, the wheat and weeds in the parable are capable of being changed into one another. A just man can become wicked, and a wicked man just. We start out as weeds but are made into God's children by baptism. And often enough, many of us spend at least part of our lives oscillating between being weeds and wheat. Let's be honest: if God ordained a world in which every time someone committed a serious sin an angel would come down and cast him into hell, there would be few of us left for the heavenly barn.

If we understand the parable in this way, suddenly the reason why God permits evil men to continue in the world and in the Church hits much closer to home. He is not just offering the good people the chance to exercise their virtues; he is also giving the bad people a chance to repent. This is what St. Peter says in his second epistle: "The Lord is not being slow about the promise, as some consider slowness, but he is being patient unto you, not wanting any to be destroyed, but [wanting] to allow space for all unto repentance" (2 Pet. 3:9). And we are likely to be among those bad people who needed more time and patience and mercy in order to repent.

So the parable is teaching us about mercy toward our neighbor by teaching us about God's mercy toward us. It is true that there are people who sin against you, who do great evil to you and your loved ones, but perhaps with a bit more time and patience and prayer and forgiveness from us, those people might find the grace of repentance and convert into God's wheat. "Blessed are the merciful, for they shall receive mercy" (Matt. 5:7): the soul you save might just be your own.

CHAPTER 4

THE WOMAN CAUGHT IN ADULTERY

Continuing the theme of God's mercy toward sinners, let us turn now to a conversation of Jesus. The conversations of Jesus are different from his parables. The parables tend to be more generic, more applicable to different persons and circumstances. They also are presented in figurative language. The conversations of Jesus, on the other hand, are more concrete and direct. They show Jesus engaged with real, historical individuals, and these encounters are not described in metaphors or figurative language. For this very reason, they can strike the reader more forcefully and immediately. The reader can put himself in the shoes of the person with whom Jesus is speaking.

There is a transforming power in the conversations of Jesus that is not found in the same way as in his parables. And although they lack some of the universal applicability of the parables, nevertheless, read in their spiritual sense, the persons and events described in each conversation can be taken as types of larger realities. An excellent example of this is found in the conversation surrounding the woman caught in adultery found in the eighth chapter of St. John's Gospel.

Jesus went to the Mount of Olives. But early in the morning he arrived again in the temple area, and all the people started coming to him, and he sat down and taught them. Then the scribes and the Pharisees brought a woman who had been caught in adultery and made her stand in the middle. They said to him, "Teacher, this woman was caught in the act of committing adultery. Now in the law, Moses commanded us to stone such women. So what do you say?" They said this to test him, so that they could have some charge to bring against him. Jesus bent down and began to write on the ground with his finger. But when they continued asking him, he straightened up and said to them, "Let the one among you who is without sin be the first to throw a stone at her."

Again he bent down and wrote on the ground. And in response, they went away one by one, beginning with the elders. So he was left alone with the woman before him. Then Jesus straightened up and said to her, "Woman, where are they? Has no one condemned you?" She replied, "No one, sir." Then Jesus said, "Neither do I condemn you. Go, and from now on do not sin anymore" (John 8:1–11).

The Context of the Conversation

The eighth chapter of John's Gospel takes place in the temple, and it begins and ends with an attempted stoning. At the beginning, the Pharisees attempt to stone the woman; by the end, there is an attempt to stone Jesus. This is already instructive, for if we begin by judging our neighbor, we may end by judging Christ himself.

The Literal Sense

The literal sense of this passage is clear enough. Recall that the literal sense of a passage is the sense directly intended and expressed by the words. The scribes and Pharisees are seeking to trap Jesus by putting him in a seemingly impossible situation. On the one hand they saw that his teaching about the mercy of God for sinners appealed to the crowds; on the other hand, the clear teaching of Moses about the just punishment due for the sin of adultery seemed to contradict Jesus' teaching about the mercy of God. He could not escape by challenging the charge of adultery, since she was "caught in the act." This, of course, leads one to wonder about where the man was, and whether this was a classic case of entrapment. Be that as it may, it seemed to them that Jesus had only three options: either he had to renounce his teaching on mercy, or reject the commandment of God, or deny that Moses was a true prophet. Any one of these would have meant doom for Jesus' ministry. So they thought . . .

The first thing to wonder about is why Jesus' message of mercy for sinners was so offensive to them. Who can get upset about someone saying that God is ready to forgive even our greatest sin? The reason is that Jesus' message of mercy included this assertion: all are in need of mercy, even the supposedly perfect scribes and Pharisees. But they wanted to be justified by their observance of the law. They wanted to be saved by their own efforts. They wanted salvation to be due to them in justice, not freely given in mercy. So they were a bunch of angry Pelagians.[15]

The Allegorical Sense

Let us look at this passage anew in its spiritual senses. Recall that the allegorical sense is the meaning of things and events insofar as they signify the truths about Christ and his

Church in the present age (for example, the truth about his Incarnation, or about the sacraments of the Church). Jesus is said to go to the Mount of Olives. In Greek the word for olive is *eluson*. That should sound familiar, since the word for mercy in Greek is *eleison*, as we sing sometimes at Mass: *Kyrie Eleison*. Any Greek speaker would have noticed the play on words. It is as if Jesus was going to the mountain of mercy, and here he is going to reveal to us how God's mercy and justice are not opposed but harmonious.

This raises an important question: How are God's justice and mercy reconcilable? I think that many Catholics, even very devout ones, and perhaps even many priests, have this idea of the relationship between God's justice and his mercy: they imagine a scale in which one side represents the demands of God's justice and the other represents the demands of his mercy. So we think: God can be merciful, but only up to a point, because then he wouldn't be just. And God can be just, but only up to a point, since then this would take away from his mercy. This idea about the relationship between God's justice and mercy is wrong on at least two counts.

First, it treats his justice and mercy as if they were opposed and mutually exclusive. But if that were the case, they could not be perfections in God, in whom everything is harmonious and unified and nothing is contrary. Second, it puts a limit on God's mercy and justice as if God can be just or merciful only in some finite degree. But this again detracts from God's unlimited goodness. We will have to see the solution to this dilemma later, and the solution will come in part by taking a more careful look at this conversation. So let's get back to the woman.

The woman, signifying sinful humanity, is set in the midst. She is in need of mercy, but her accusers demand justice. There seems no way out. How can God be just and yet merciful toward our fallen human race? But then something wonderful happens. Jesus bends down and begins to write in the earth. And this is all done in silence. What does this mean? St. Thomas Aquinas, with the keenness of his mystical insight, says that this action signifies that God in his mercy is stooping down to assist sinful humanity. In fact, he says, whenever Jesus stoops down it signifies an act of God's mercy, and whenever he stands up straight it signifies an act of God's justice. For the Greek word for justice literally means "uprightness." It is the same word in the Greek for what Jesus is doing by standing upright!

But what does the writing in the earth signify? Once again, Thomas penetrates into the mystery. The Greek word there is *katagraphein*. It appears only once in the New Testament, and that is here. It doesn't exactly mean "write"—that would be *graphein*—but *katagraphein* means "to write down into," or simply "to engrave." And although it doesn't appear elsewhere in the New Testament, it does appear sometimes in the Greek version of the Old Testament, and almost always in relation to a single event: when God engraves the commandments with his finger in the tablets of stone. So the Fathers of the Church say that Jesus is here writing the commandments into the earth.

But in its spiritual sense, says Thomas, it signifies the mystery of the Incarnation—when by the finger of God, the Holy Spirit,[16] the eternal Word was written into our human nature, as Isaiah the prophet once wrote: "Let the heavens rain down the Just One and the earth bring forth a Savior."[17] The earth is a fit symbol for human nature since our nature was taken from the earth.[18] And all this is done in silence to signify the ineffability of this mystery.[19] It is as if Jesus is saying to the scribes and Pharisees: "Yes, according to Moses she ought to be condemned and stoned to death, but that was before mercy was available through the Incarnation. Therefore, there is now hope for sinners."

But the scribes and Pharisees do not understand the mystery, and they break the reverent silence with a cacophony of cries: they want justice, they want blood. *And as they continued to ask him, he stood up and said to them, "Let him who is without sin among you be the first to throw a stone at her."* By straightening up, Jesus is now signifying his justice. They have asked for justice and justice they will receive, but now it is they who also stand accused. Jesus does not deny that she deserves death, but he adds to this that so do these scribes and Pharisees. This causes them to place themselves in the shoes of the accused. Perhaps they would have stoned her anyway if they did not think this would cause them to lose the favor of the crowds. Pride sometimes even feigns humility in order to achieve its aims.

But what happens next? Jesus stoops down again, as if to offer mercy to the newly accused. And this time he begins to write again, but the word now is *graphein*. He is not engraving but simply writing lightly in the earth. And the Fathers of the Church tell us that now he is writing their sins, but lightly as if to indicate that these can be easily wiped away if only they will accept that they too need God's mercy. Jesus is revealing to them that he knows their hidden sins too. *But when they heard it, they went away, one by one, beginning with the eldest, and Jesus was left alone with the woman standing before him.* The eldest was most aware of the sins of a long life, for he had "grown old in his sins" (Dan. 13:52). And therefore, faced with the decision to admit and confess his sins before the people, or to remain in his feigned innocence, he flees from the mercy offered to him by Christ. And so it was with all the others, except the woman, who no longer had any claim to innocence since her sin had been made public.

Then what happens last of all? Jesus stands up again to render his just judgment: *Jesus looked up and said to her, "Woman, where are they? Has no one condemned you?" She said, "No one, Lord."* She stands because she has been justified by the mercy of Christ, not because she was justified by her own merits. Hence she hears the sentence: *And Jesus said, "Neither do I condemn you; go, and do sin no more."*

To recap the allegorical sense: the woman represents sinful humanity in need of God's mercy. The scribes and Pharisees signify those who accuse us, whether they be our sins, or the demons. Jesus stooping down signifies God showing mercy. Jesus writing (or rather engraving) in the earth the first time signifies the Holy Spirit irrevocably writing the word of God into the earth of our human nature at the moment of the Incarnation. Jesus standing up signifies God exercising justice. The woman standing alone at the end signifies humanity justified by God's grace, now free from accusation and guilt.

The Anagogical Sense

That was the allegorical sense of the passage, but there is also an anagogical sense: namely, how it signifies the things of the next life. And here we can reread the passage as referring to the final judgment when all are brought before the judgment seat of Christ. Jesus goes to the Mount of Olives, because just as he ascended from there he will return again to the same place to judge the living and the dead.[20] And at the general judgment all the people are brought before him, he takes his judgment seat and teaches them—that is, makes manifest the whole truth about human hearts.

There are two kinds of people brought to Jesus: not sinners and innocent, for all will be sinners. Rather, there are those who despite their past sins desire God's glory first and care not about their own glory, and those who care first about their own glory and wish to pretend to be innocent. Once a young man came to me to ask my opinion about a sin he had committed. He wanted to know if I thought the sin had been serious. After he described it, I told him that I thought it was likely that it was a serious sin, and he was just heartbroken because he had tried so hard to stay free from serious sin for his whole life. But the Holy Spirit gave me just the right words at that moment. I said to him: "What would you prefer, that your innocence be glorified at the final judgment because you never committed a serious sin, or that God's mercy be glorified because he forgave you your sin?" He immediately cheered up and said, "You're right, father! I would much rather have God's mercy be glorified than my innocence!"

At the final judgment, all will be given a choice to confess their sins and receive mercy or to pretend to hide their sins and flee from the mercy of Christ. And those who care more for God's glory will want everyone to know their sins. They will want everyone to know how merciful God has been toward them. But the proud who prefer their own apparent glory to God's glory will flee even to the depths of hell to avoid the shame of seeing their sins made public. But those who have nothing to lose, whose sins are already made known, will hear the final command: go and never sin again; that is, go into heaven where it will no longer be possible for you to sin.

God's Justice and Mercy

I said above that it is a false view to think of God's justice and mercy as being opposed or in competition. In his *Summa Theologiae,* St. Thomas rejects a similar view about the relationship between God's justice and mercy.[21] When considering the sin of presumption, he raises the objection that it seems impossible to commit the sin of presumption, since this sin involves trusting too much in God's mercy. But it is impossible to trust too much in God's mercy. Therefore, it is impossible to commit the sin of presumption.

Thomas responds with a wisdom that can only belong to a saint: one who commits the sin of presumption does not trust too much, but too little in God's mercy. For the presumptuous man wants to be freed from the punishment due to his sins, but not from the sin itself; that is the far greater evil. But God in his mercy wants to free us not only from punishment but also from sin, since this is to take away a much greater misery. That is very beautiful and very insightful. So long as we want to be freed from our sins, we are not guilty of the sin of presumption. Presumption happens when we want to cling to our sins, when we want to resist God's mercy, which desires to free us from this greatest of all evils.

Once I was at the bedside of a very good woman as she neared death, and a fear overcame her that perhaps she was being presumptuous in thinking that God would forgive her. I told her that so long as she wanted to be freed from her sins, she had no reason to fear that she was guilty of presumption. And she understood that the devil was trying to destroy her confidence in God's mercy, and her peace of soul was restored.

How are God's justice and mercy related? If we inquire more carefully, we see that God's justice is ordered to and for the sake of God's mercy. Recall that mercy is God's goodness looked at from the perspective of removing our misery or defects. And there are two great defects from which we suffer: sin and our ignorance of sin. Take the case of a man who is sick with a deadly disease. The disease itself is evil, since it can kill him. But if he is unaware that he has this disease, this is also evil, since he will never seek a remedy. That is why pain can in some sense be good, since it tells us there is something wrong with us that needs to be fixed. If someone is in sin, this is already very bad, but if he is also ignorant of his sin, this is even worse. He is like the man who has a deadly disease but will not go to see a doctor, since he thinks there is nothing wrong with him.

This is where God's justice comes in. By his justice, God frees us from the evil of ignorance of sin, and by his mercy God frees us from the sin itself. St. Paul says to the Romans: "By the works of the law, no flesh shall be justified before [God]. For by the law is the knowledge of sin" (Rom. 3:20). In other words, the law that was an expression of God's justice was instituted not to take sin away, but to take away the ignorance of sin (our ignorance and the ignorance of others as well, as when the punishment given to some is a warning to others).

So also in our own spiritual lives. God gives us a knowledge of our sinfulness, and this can be painful. At these times we think of ourselves as being subject to God's justice, to punishment and wrath. God takes away from us some created good: our possessions, people we love, our health, our interior consolations. When he does this, we come to realize how attached we were to these creatures. We realize that we were looking for happiness in them, and so the depth of our misery is made known to us. We can even feel rejected by God at these times. But this exercise of God's justice is for the sake of his mercy, for only when we come to know and acknowledge our sinfulness are we in a position to ask for forgiveness and mercy. And when we experience the Lord taking away our sins, we experience this as an act of his mercy.

In my own meditations, I have found a beautiful example of this in Psalm 107, which describes four groups of people: those looking for a city to dwell in (those outside the Church); those in prison for defying God's commands (those in the Church but in mortal sin); those who are sick and come close to death (those in venial sin); and those who cast out into the deep waters (those apostolic men and women who strive for sanctity). In each case God allows them to see their misery so that they might call upon him: "They cried to the Lord in their distress, he answered and saved them." God's justice prepares the way for his mercy.

Fortunately, God usually reveals our misery gradually, because he knows well our weaknesses. He will not break us, even if he puts us through a great trial. One saint said that God briefly revealed to him his misery, and had God not supported him by the power of his grace, he would have despaired instantly. So God is gentle with us as with little children. Someone might ask: Why isn't it enough to just admit we are sinners, like at the *Confiteor* at Mass? Why does God have to cause us so much suffering and pain to reveal our sinfulness to us? One reason is that until we actually experience our sinfulness directly, we will always underestimate it, just as one who has never directly experienced poverty or intense physical suffering tends to underestimate the struggles of those who are destitute and suffering. It is like the case of a man who has a debt of a million dollars, and someone comes and pays the debt for him; but the problem is that the man thought his debt was only a thousand dollars. He will be grateful to the man who paid his debt, but nowhere near as grateful as he ought to be.

So it is with us: until we experientially know firsthand the full depths of our sinfulness we will simply not be as grateful to God as we ought to be when he shows us his mercy. Simply acknowledging that we are sinners at the *Confiteor* every Mass is not enough, since all of us greatly underestimate the debt of our sins. In fact, the process of growing in holiness is experienced internally not as becoming holier, but as becoming more aware of our sinfulness. When a man with dirty clothes comes closer to the light, he sees those stains more clearly precisely because he is closer to the light. So too, the closer we come to the light who is Christ, the more we become aware of our sinfulness, even though we are closer to Christ than before.

Becoming a saint is a humiliating journey, and it does not feel like a triumphal procession.[22] Yet there is something beautiful about realizing that, with all our sins, we are cherished by the Lord. So do not run from the light on account of your sins, do not say "Depart from me, for I am a sinful man." Rather, run to the physician, you who are sick; run to the fount of mercy, you who need mercy.

Understood in this way, the relationship between justice and mercy is not seen as a relationship of contrariety, but rather of harmony. Mercy presupposes justice, and justice is for the sake of mercy. Justice manifests the need for mercy, and mercy heals the need justice reveals. It is not a question of God being too just or too merciful, like two sides of a scale. Increasing justice does not mean reducing mercy. The greatness of God's justice does not oppose the greatness of his mercy, but rather great mercy presupposes great justice, since unless one learns through justice one's need for mercy, mercy will not be experienced as mercy. And unless God's justice be great, the greatness of his mercy will not be understood.

Hence, it is no mercy to leave someone in ignorance of their sinfulness. The man who lets his blind friend walk into a ditch because he didn't want to hurt his feelings by telling him he was walking the wrong way is not showing mercy. St. Augustine puts it this way in his Rule: "And do not think you are uncharitable for pointing out your brother's fault. For if your brother had a bodily wound that he wanted to hide because he feared the cure, would it not be cruel of you to keep silent and a kindness to make it known? How much greater is your obligation to manifest his spiritual wound, lest he grow more corrupt in his heart?"

All the faithful have an obligation in charity to practice fraternal correction; and priests especially must imitate this action of divine justice in their preaching, in the confessional, and in spiritual direction. They must remember that everything is for the sake of making God's mercy available to the sinner, and they must avoid a false "pastoral" approach that refuses to tell people about their sins, or to act as if their objectively sinful state makes no difference. So the priest must tell people when they are sinning; this is justice. But the priest should at the same time make clear that mercy is always available for the repentant.

Withholding saving truth from someone is not mercy and it is not pastoral: no good shepherd lets his sheep stay lost! If there is such a thing as saving truth, then there must be such a thing as damning error or ignorance. We can't hide behind the false mercy of invincible ignorance, as if people will be saved by their ignorance. Jesus did not say, "You shall not know the truth, but invincible ignorance shall set you free." The truth is that our inclination to leave someone alone and not bring up their faults often has more to do with self-love than love of neighbor. We don't want them to dislike us, so we leave them in danger for the sake of being liked.

Yet just as God does not reveal our sins and defects to us all at once and in their full ugliness, so too the priest should gradually and gently reveal the faults of his flock. Begin with the absolutely essential problems, the big faults, and then from there address the other things that need to be corrected. Usually corrections should be made gently, as St. Paul admonishes: "Brethren, if a man be overtaken in any fault, you who are spiritual, instruct such a one in a spirit of meekness, considering yourself lest you also be tempted" (Gal. 6:1). In fact, we know we are correcting someone in the right spirit when we are not looking for all his faults but for reasons why he might be less blameworthy; and when we are more willing to do penance for our brother's faults than to punish them. When Jesus sees our faults, the first thing he thinks is not "how can I punish them?" but "how can I help them?" And Jesus is always willing to take the punishment due for our sins upon himself.

Paul implies that we should do the same when he continues his admonition by saying: "Bear one another's burdens, and thus you will fulfill the law of Christ" (Gal. 6:2). There are rare cases when corrections should be forceful: when you are morally certain that the person is sinning out of malice. But we should be very hesitant to assume this: most sins are ones of weakness and ignorance, even habitual sins. St. Alphonsus teaches that excessive harshness in administering a correction is much worse than over-lenience.[23] This is how we ought to be truly pastoral, not by letting our sheep remain lost, but by gently laying them upon our shoulders and carrying them back to the flock instead of driving them back by harsh blows. Augustine has such beautiful advice about this in his sermon on pastors[24] (which is read over the course of nearly two weeks in the office of readings).

CHAPTER 5

THE SAMARITAN WOMAN AT THE WELL

One of the most remarkable conversions that Jesus brought about in his lifetime was the conversion of a Samaritan woman in John 4. And through her, he prepared the way of conversion for many Samaritans. Man teaches through external words and signs, but God is able to instruct and enlighten from within. This conversation relates how the divinity and the humanity of our Savior cooperate in marvelous fashion to bring about the conversion of a Samaritan woman. In some way, this conversion serves as a model or archetype of the conversion of every soul, as a careful reading of the text will confirm.

> He had to pass through Samaria. So he came to a town of Samaria called Sychar, near the plot of land that Jacob had given to his son Joseph. Jacob's well was there. Jesus, tired from his journey, sat down there at the well. It was about noon. A woman of Samaria came to draw water. Jesus said to her, "Give me a drink." His disciples had gone into the town to buy food.

The Samaritan woman said to him, "How can you, a Jew, ask me, a Samaritan woman, for a drink?" (For Jews use nothing in common with Samaritans.) Jesus answered and said to her, "If you knew the gift of God and who is saying to you, 'Give me a drink,' you would have asked him and he would have given you living water." [The woman] said to him, "Sir, you do not even have a bucket and the well is deep; where then can you get this living water? Are you greater than our father Jacob, who gave us this well and drank from it himself with his children and his flocks?"

Jesus answered and said to her, "Everyone who drinks this water will be thirsty again; but whoever drinks the water I shall give will never thirst; the water I shall give will become in him a spring of water welling up to eternal life." The woman said to him, "Sir, give me this water, so that I may not be thirsty or have to keep coming here to draw water." Jesus said to her, "Go call your husband and come back." The woman answered and said to him, "I do not have a husband." Jesus answered her, "You are right in saying, 'I do not have a husband.' For you have had five husbands, and the one you have now is not your husband. What you have said is true." The woman said to him, "Sir, I can see that you are a prophet. Our ancestors worshipped on this mountain; but you people say that the place to worship is in Jerusalem."

Jesus said to her, "Believe me, woman, the hour is coming when you will worship the Father neither on this mountain nor in Jerusalem. You people worship what you do not understand; we worship what we understand, because salvation is from the Jews. But the hour is coming, and is now here, when true worshipers will worship the Father in spirit and truth; and indeed the Father seeks such people to worship him. God is spirit, and those who worship him must worship in spirit and truth." The woman said to him, "I know that the Messiah is coming, the one called the Anointed; when he comes, he will tell us everything." Jesus said to her, "I am he, the one who is speaking with you."

At that moment his disciples returned, and were amazed that he was talking with a woman, but still no one said, "What are you looking for?" or "Why are you talking with her?" The woman left her water jar and went into the town and said to the people, "Come see a man who told me everything I have done. Could he possibly be the Messiah?" They went out of the town and came to him.

Meanwhile, the disciples urged him, "Rabbi, eat." But he said to them, "I have food to eat of which you do not know." So the disciples said to one another, "Could someone have brought him something to eat?" Jesus said to them, "My food is to do the will of the one who sent me and to finish his work. Do you not say, 'In four months the harvest will be here'? I tell you, look up and see the fields ripe for the harvest. The reaper is already receiving his payment and gathering crops for eternal life, so that the sower and reaper can rejoice together. For here the saying is verified that 'One sows and another reaps.' I sent you to reap what you have not worked for; others have done the work, and you are sharing the fruits of their work."

Many of the Samaritans of that town began to believe in him because of the word of the woman who testified, "He told me everything I have done." When the Samaritans came to him, they invited him to stay with them; and he stayed there two days. Many more began to believe in him because of his word, and they said to the woman, "We no longer believe because of your word; for we have heard for ourselves, and we know that this is truly the Savior of the world" (John 4:4–42).

The Context of the Conversation

St. John tells us that the occasion of this conversation was that Jesus was on his way to Galilee from Judea and so had to pass through Samaria (Samaria is just north of Judea, and Galilee is just north of Samaria). That explains why Jesus is in Samaria in the first place. But John also mentions something else: the reason Jesus left Judea for Galilee was that the Pharisees were alerted to the fact that Jesus was making so many disciples, even more than John the Baptist. This likely provoked their envy and anger, so Jesus left Judea for a time. But did that mean that Jesus stopped making converts and disciples? No.

And this is where the conversation with the Samaritan woman comes in. Jesus wants to continue evangelizing, even beyond the district of the Jews. And so he begins this conversation in order to produce an abundant harvest of souls for the kingdom of God: "Do you not say, 'In four months the harvest will be here'? I tell you, look up and see the fields ripe for the harvest. The reaper is already receiving his payment and gathering crops for eternal life" (John 4:35–36). So this conversation is about evangelization.

Being Evangelized by the Conversation with the Samaritan Woman

The first thing that must happen when we read this conversation is that we have to place ourselves in the person of the Samaritan woman. We have to permit Jesus' words to evangelize us, to bring about conversion in us. The conversion of this woman takes place in several stages or steps, and so we must walk along the same path, following the same steps she does in order to reap the fruit of conversion through this conversation.

We should notice too that this conversation has such extraordinary power because it is Christ, the God-man, who speaks. The power of God to move the human heart, and the power of Jesus' words to communicate divine truths, is made manifest through a conversion that is both complete and sudden. For in no other way can we explain how a pagan woman living in sin is moved to confess Jesus as the Christ, as the Savior of the world, after a short conversation. And it is certain that her conversion is not simply a matter of words, for she immediately goes forth to confess Jesus to her people and in this way brings a multitude to salvation.

We too are in need of such a conversion, a conversion that is sudden and complete, a conversion that impels us to confess Jesus as the Christ and to bring others to him. How was this simple woman, so trapped in her sins, able to obtain such a tremendous infusion of grace? Perhaps if we could find out we might be able to imitate her and thus obtain for ourselves this same grace. Let us prayerfully investigate the scriptures and ask our Lord for the gift of understanding from his Holy Spirit so that we might be able to unlock the treasures that the words of the scriptures hold.

The woman has come to the well to draw water. She seeks no spiritual drink, but only drink that satisfies the flesh. For as the prophet Jeremiah said, "My people have done two evils: they have forsaken me, the fountain of living water, and have dug for themselves cisterns, broken cisterns that can hold no water" (Jer. 2:13). That is, they have turned away from God, the fountain of life—that spiritual drink which satisfies eternally—and have turned toward creatures that cannot satisfy. For although creatures seem to hold life, and satisfy us for a time, like broken cisterns we soon find them empty and unsatisfying. She comes to the well seemingly without a desire for God.

But behold, Jesus is already there at the well. She has not come to seek him, but he has come to seek her. Though she could not ascend to him, he has come down to her. She knew not that she longed for anything but earthly drink, and so Jesus condescends to sit beside the misplaced object of her desire, so that as she seeks for physical drink, she might find that true spiritual fountain. When she arrives at the well, she does not speak to Jesus, perhaps because she knows well that she is not worthy of his conversation. He is a Jew, she a Samaritan. He is a man, she is a woman. He is a rabbi, she is uneducated. It is hardly possible that even if she so desired, she could speak to him; nor could she hope that he would speak to her. And yet this is what he does. He has first loved her and so he speaks to her first.

If we are to be converted, this is the first truth we must grasp: even the desire for conversion begins with God. We cannot seek this grace of conversion unless God himself has already found us. He seeks us out first; he waits for us beside our petty loves and carnal desires; he speaks to us first. "Turn to us, O Lord, and we shall be converted" (Lam. 5:21).

When Jesus speaks, what does he say? Does he first reprove or condemn her? No, for the "Son of Man has come not to destroy souls, but to save" (Luke 9:55). He asks her for a drink of water. He asks her to perform an act of mercy, to give to him of her worldly goods. This is how God deals with us, how he gently lays us upon his shoulders when we are lost. He asks us to give him some small bit of the perishable things that we love too much, and in this way he gradually and gently redirects our love toward him and away from those perishable goods.

This is the second lesson we must learn. God wills us to come to know him especially through acts of mercy. This is the quick and sure path to conversion: "Blessed are the merciful, for they shall obtain mercy" (Matt: 5:7). For when we show mercy to our neighbors, we give truly unto God: "Whatsoever you did for the least of my brethren, you did also for me" (Matt. 25:40). For the price of temporal things we purchase for ourselves eternal treasures.

At first, the woman is taken aback by his question. She fears to enter into conversation with Jesus since she perceives that his station is above hers. She wonders that he should need or want anything from her, and moreover she has misunderstood his request. For he sought to be refreshed more by her love than by the water within the well: "I seek not the gift, but the fruit that may abound to your account" (Phil. 4:17). And so he begins to reveal this truth to her, yet still in terms that she might understand: *If you knew the gift of God* [that is, the Holy Spirit] *and who is saying to you, "Give me a drink," you would have asked him and he would have given you living water.*

This is the third lesson. It is not that God wills our conversion so that he might have something from us, but rather that we might receive something much greater than we already possess from him. We should not be afraid of opening the door to Christ! He comes only to give, not to take away. And what he seems to take away, he replaces with the goods we truly desire.

Having heard of Jesus' desire to give a gift to her, her fears are somewhat allayed, and she is encouraged to speak at greater length with Jesus. Within her soul, the first vestiges of spiritual longing begin to surface. Yet her mind is still clouded with carnal thoughts, and, thinking still that he is speaking about the water in the well, she protests that he has nothing with which to draw it, unless, perhaps, he is greater than Jacob who gave them this well. Notice that she has begun to sense something in Jesus that she had not noticed before. She seems to consider that perhaps there is one greater than Jacob here. Yet because of the darkness of her mind, she cannot penetrate the true meaning of his words nor discover yet his true greatness.

Jesus tries to explain the true nature of this water to her and the true identity of him who offers it: *Everyone who drinks this water will be thirsty again; but whoever drinks the water I shall give will never thirst; the water I shall give will become in him a spring of water welling up to eternal life.* She desires to have this living water, but only so that she may no longer feel thirst or be bothered by the labor of drawing water: *Sir, give me this water, so that I may not be thirsty or have to keep coming here to draw.* She recognizes the worth of eternal things, yet she seeks them still in a temporal way.

And so Jesus begins to purify her so that she might be given light to understand his true meaning. This first purification is a purification of the flesh, a purification that can only be accomplished through humiliation and self-knowledge. He asks her to call her husband so that she might understand the misery of her condition. She suddenly reflects within her soul upon her slavery to carnal desires, and at the same time Jesus reveals to her that he has known this all along. Just as he was not repulsed by her being a Samaritan woman, he is not repulsed by her sins. No, he has chosen to come close to her knowing full well her sins; he has chosen to enter into conversation with her knowing the entire depths of her misery. She is utterly humiliated, yet together with this humiliation comes a great security: the certitude that he has entered into conversation with her knowing her as she really is. Suddenly, the light of divine truth breaks forth into her soul as she begins to recognize Jesus for who he really is. *Sir, I can see that you are a prophet.*

This moment in their conversation reminds me of a conversation I once had with a young man whom I knew well. I was officiating at a wedding, and this young man was present with his girlfriend as a guest. During the reception we talked privately for a bit and I asked him how things were going with his girlfriend. Much to my surprise, he said, "Father, things are terrible: she's in love with another man."

This astonished me because I had seen them smiling and laughing and having a good time together at the reception. I asked him to explain. He said, "Father, the entire time I have been dating her I have been hiding my faults and defects from her because I am afraid she wouldn't want to date me if she knew my problems. I have put up a façade, and she's not in love with the real me: she's in love with the man I am pretending to be."

The truth is, unless we are loved by someone who really knows who we are, with our faults and problems, we cannot experience being truly loved. It is exactly this barrier that Jesus removes by revealing to the Samaritan woman that he knows her worst sins. She can finally experience being loved by someone as she truly is. And God has to remove that same barrier from between him and you. This is the fourth lesson.

There is also a fifth lesson here: God wills to give us eternal goods, but not so that we might love them carnally. Our conversion must involve a purification from our fleshly desires so that we might love spiritual goods for their own sake, not simply for the benefit that accrues to our flesh. And God effects this conversion in us precisely by humiliations and self-knowledge. Together with this self-knowledge comes a deeper security, a more profound knowledge of Christ as one who does not shun us in our sinfulness but seeks us out and desires to be with us precisely because of our sinfulness. We can finally experience being loved as we truly are.

Having been thus purified, the woman now begins to perceive the importance of spiritual realities. Her conversation takes a markedly different turn as she understands that it is the worship of God that is at issue, not simply the satisfying of bodily thirst. And so she brings a difficulty to Jesus: *Our ancestors worshipped on this mountain; but you people say that the place to worship is in Jerusalem.* It is as if she is suddenly reminded of the importance of a difficulty that had once troubled her long ago, but that she had pushed out of her mind by immersing herself in carnal pleasures. Having been freed from the inordinate attachment to these pleasures, her mind instinctively turns again to this problem.

Yet the question itself betrays a certain spiritual blindness. For as of yet she still does not understand the nature of spiritual things. The things of the spirit have not bodies, nor are they circumscribed by place. And so the Spirit of God need not be worshipped in this place or that, but from the spirit that is within each man. There is yet a further purification needed, and this is the purification of the spirit. And so Jesus begins to illumine her mind with his teaching. He does not illumine her as one might expect. He does not teach her in such a way that she can easily understand his meaning and judge it by her own reason. Rather, he leaves her in the darkness of faith: *Believe me, woman . . . you people worship what you do not understand.* Jesus confronts her with truths beyond her capacity to grasp and demands her assent.

This is the essence of the purification of the spirit, the dark night of faith that must come before the light of glory. In her ignorance, overwhelmed by the brightness of divine truth, the woman humbly acknowledges her need for a teacher, her need for the teacher of all truth: *I know that the Messiah is coming, the one called the Anointed; when he comes, he will tell us everything.* "Be not called Teacher, one alone is your Teacher, the Christ" (Matt. 23:10). Having been thus purified, the woman now realizes that she had come to the well all along to seek the Christ. But she did not know that he was waiting there and already speaking with her. And so Jesus, having awakened within the woman her true and original desire, fulfils it when he says, *I am he, the one who is speaking with you.* It is no mere man of great importance who speaks to you, but your Savior and God. Though men do not deem you worthy of conversation, your God has desired to converse with you in his love.

The words said about the blind man of John 9:37–8 could aptly be applied to the Samaritan woman as well: "You have both seen him and it is he who is speaking with you. And he said, 'I believe, Lord.' And falling down, he adored him." This is the perfection of the contemplative life: to converse with the God one knows and loves.

This is the sixth lesson. Complete conversion does not come without unshakable faith and a loving trust. And yet when all is said and done, God himself must bring to completion the work he began within us. Only thus can we come to the point of realizing our complete dependence upon God. It remains his free and loving gift to reveal himself fully to us.

It might seem that her conversion is complete, and so nothing remains to be said. But the evangelist is careful to relate that the woman is not content to remain in conversation with Jesus. She has been purified to such an extent that she no longer desires him for herself alone, but for all. And therefore, she does not linger with Jesus but goes immediately to her countrymen that they too might know him This is all the more remarkable, as among her countrymen were her five ex-husbands.

Yet she does not fear their scorn, nor the scorn of all those who know her past: for she is not preaching herself, but Christ. "For what we preach is not ourselves, but Jesus Christ as Lord, with ourselves as your servants for Jesus' sake" (2 Cor. 4:5). She does not preach him as her savior, but as the savior of the world. And she does not wish them to depend upon her word alone, but she brings them to Jesus so that they may see and have Jesus as their own: "He must increase, while I must decrease" (John 3:30).

This is the last lesson. Total conversion demands that God be loved in such a way that even the sweetness of contemplation must be subordinated to the divine will for the sake of the common good. We do not love God as ours alone, as if he were our private good to the exclusion of others. That would ultimately amount to self-love. Instead, we love God in such a way that we desire that his goodness should be shared with all, and this desire outweighs even our own desire for possessing him. It was this sentiment that caused St. Paul to exclaim: "I would that I should be anathema from Christ for the sake of my brethren!" (Rom. 9:3).

The Allegorical Sense

As with the many other passages, this one also contains a profound spiritual sense that we should not pass over in silence. St. John discovered in the events of this conversation that the crucified Savior was hidden within them. It was not merely the words of Jesus that brought about this woman's conversion: for this entire conversation was a sacrament of the coming Passion, of Jesus crucified as the source of the Holy Spirit, by whose grace we are converted.

Consider the details recorded about Jesus in this Gospel. He has not come some short distance, but he has come from far away, and is weary from the journey. This seems to be a fulfillment of the words of Proverbs: "Like cold water to a thirsty soul, so is the gospel from a far country" (Prov. 25:25). He has paid a great price to seek you out. Notice the circumstances of his coming: it is about the sixth hour, and his disciples have left him, and he thirsts. The evangelist has noted these details so that we might be led to understand the spiritual significance of this meeting. For when the Word was made flesh and dwelt among us, he came from far off—for divinity is infinitely separated from humanity. And he is wearied from his journey, since he has assumed "the likeness of sinful flesh" (Rom. 8:3) and the burdens consequent upon our feeble humanity. And when he was crucified, it was the sixth hour, and his disciples had left him, and he thirsts.

There are already three parallels there. But we can add two more: at his side here and at the cross, there stands a woman together with the beloved disciple (who must have been there to record this conversation). And from his pierced side flowed a fountain of living water; that is, the Holy Spirit. This entire passage, then, is meant to be understood as a foreshadowing, even a sacrament, of the Crucifixion.

Therefore we can look back at this entire conversation as if it were the conversation between Christ and his Church as he hangs upon the cross. Each of us can see ourselves in the Samaritan woman as we look upon the crucified Savior. From the cross Jesus leads us to conversion: conversion from our sins to love of him, and from love of him to love of neighbor.

Where are you in this conversation? Are you at the beginning, still clinging to your water pot, hoping to find happiness in the fleeting pleasures of this world? Have you come to recognize Jesus as someone important, but not yet as your savior? Do you seek eternal things, but in an earthly way? Are you struggling to accept the teachings of Christ you can't understand? Are you desirous of loving conversation with Jesus, but not yet zealous to bring others to him? Wherever you are in this conversation, Jesus wants you to trust him so you can take the next step in loving him. Your sins do not scare him away or repulse him. Nor can you use them as excuses not to evangelize. For you are not bringing them to you, but to Jesus.

Evangelizing by Means of the Conversation with the Samaritan Woman

Jesus surprises even his own closest friends and disciples when he seeks out this Samaritan woman. He does not consider her unworthy to hear the Gospel. This woman lacked an education and lacked social status. She was a heretic and a serial fornicator. Yet Jesus spoke to her and deemed her worthy to be an apostle. Similarly for us, we must consider no one unworthy of evangelizing. And just as Jesus did, we should begin this process by encouraging works of mercy. We should gradually help them to overcome their fleshly attachments so that they might see more and more clearly the goods of the spirit. We ourselves must be authentic witnesses of these goods, free from carnal desires; and, like Jesus, we should assure them of the beauty and goodness of a life lived in the Spirit.

It is not enough to tell others that they must give up their worldly goods. We must also promise them better, more satisfying goods. We must radiate that charity which assures them that we still desire to enter into communion with them despite their sinful lives and attachments. Our preaching of the need for conversion from sin must never appear as a rejection of the sinner. And once we have won them over for Christ, we must form them to become evangelists too. For only in this way will their faith and love reach fulfilment.

CHAPTER 6

THE GOOD SAMARITAN

The famous parable of the Good Samaritan is found only in the Gospel according to St. Luke. It speaks especially of works of mercy, a theme dear to the heart of Luke and his companion St. Paul, who was especially mindful of the poor (see Galatians 2:10).

A certain man went down from Jerusalem to Jericho and fell among robbers who also stripped him, and having wounded him went away, leaving him half-dead. And it happened that a certain priest went down the same way: and seeing him, passed by. In like manner also, a Levite, when he was near the place and saw him, passed by. But a certain Samaritan being on his journey came near him, and seeing him was moved with compassion. And going up to him, bound up his wounds, pouring in oil and wine, and setting him upon his own beast, brought him to an inn and took care of him.

And the next day, he took out two coins and gave them to the innkeeper and said, "Whatsoever you shall spend over and above I, at my return, will repay you." Which of these three in your opinion was neighbor to him that fell among the robbers? But he said, "He that showed mercy to him." And Jesus said to him: "Go and do likewise" (Luke 10:30–37).

The Context of the Parable

Jesus told this parable in response to a question by a teacher of the law who was testing Jesus about the conditions for possessing eternal life. The lawyer correctly identifies the great commandments of love of God and love of neighbor, but then, in an attempt to justify himself, he asks for a clarification about who is his neighbor. It is remarkable that Jesus answers his question so beautifully and profoundly even though his motivations are not upright. Jesus is the sower who sows the good seed even on bad soil. The lawyer wants to appear knowledgeable and deserving of the title "teacher." But Jesus emphasizes the fact that it is not knowledge of the commandments but doing the commandments that results in eternal life. Mercy is not just about words, it is even more about deeds.

The Literal Sense

The literal sense of this parable instructs us that our neighbors are not restricted to those who hold the same beliefs as we do. Certainly the priest and the Levite were authorities and knowledgeable about the law of God, yet that knowledge did not make them a neighbor to the fallen man.

On the other hand, the Samaritan—who held not only different beliefs, but false beliefs—was moved with compassion, and through this compassion was moved to action. This underscores the spiritual universality of the new priesthood (whether the ministerial priesthood or the priesthood of all the baptized), which is truly universal, truly catholic, not bound to one people nor giving preference to carnal relations. Deeds of love and mercy are not restricted to those who are always correct, and it is compassion and the deeds that flow from it that determine who our neighbor is. Our neighbor is anyone who does deeds of mercy or anyone to whom we can show mercy.

The Spiritual Sense

It is worthwhile to pause and reflect more profoundly on the spiritual sense of this parable, since it is a summary of the entire history of salvation. *A certain man went down from Jerusalem to Jericho.* In its spiritual sense, this *certain man* was Adam. For in ancient Hebrew and Aramaic (the language Jesus would have been speaking) the word for "man" is the name "Adam." Adam was at first in *Jerusalem*, which means "the city of peace"—namely, the garden of paradise—but then he *went down into Jericho*—that is, into the state of corruption. St. Augustine observes that Jericho means "moon," which, by its waxing and waning, indicates the mutability of man's present state.[25] And he *fell among robbers.* These robbers signify the devil and his angels, who *stripped him* of the garment of charity and original justice. For charity is often represented in Scripture under the figure of a garment, as when St. Paul says, "Over all these, put on charity" (Col. 3:14). *And they left him wounded* with the wound of original sin and the wounds of actual sins.

After this, they *departed leaving him half-dead.* The demons abandoned man since they had no interest in him save to lure him into sin, though they feigned interest in his welfare at first. This is how the demons tempt us: by pretending to have our best interests at heart, but then after we sin they show their true colors. After the fall, man is said to be *half-dead*, either because, "man after sin is said to be half-dead because his soul is immortal, but his body mortal, so that the half of man is under death;"[26] or because having lost the

life of God in their souls, men still retained the life of their
bodies for a time, so while their bodies were alive, their
souls were dead.

And a certain priest, representing the priesthood of the
Old Covenant, *came down that way by chance*; that is, with
remedies that bore no intrinsic power in themselves to heal
man's fallen state. For the sacrifices of the old law were mere
signs of future realities and bore no intrinsic relation to the
wound that needed to be healed. Thus it is said to happen
by chance, since those things that are not related essentially
to a thing happen to it by chance. *And he passed by on the
other side*, for the sacrifices of the old law were ineffectual of
themselves for taking away sin, "for it was impossible that
the blood of bulls and goats should take away sin" (Heb.
10:4). And therefore these sacrifices and the priesthood as-
sociated with them passed by as being established for a time
only before the coming of Christ.

Likewise a Levite—that is, one knowledgeable in the
law—*came and looked upon him, and passed by on the other side*;
that is, the law made known to man his sin (so that it is said
to look upon him) but could not provide a remedy for it (so
that it is said to pass him by). "For no man will be justified
in his sight by works of the law; since through the law comes
knowledge of sin" (Rom. 3:20). Thus also, the old law was
in effect for a time, until it was fulfilled in Christ. And so
both the former priesthood and law were unable to assist
man in his condition of original sin, since for this grace was
necessary. Only the new priesthood and the new law is able
to heal the wound of original sin.

And a certain Samaritan—that is, Christ—*came down to him*.
Jesus was called a Samaritan for good reason: for he came
from a foreign country "above" Judah (namely, his heavenly
homeland). Thus, when the Lord was accused by the Jews of

having a devil and being a Samaritan, he refuted them with regard to the first accusation but not the second (John 8:48 and following) to signify that he was indeed from a foreign land. He testified this to Pontius Pilate when he said, "My kingdom is not of this world" (John 18:36). And Jesus is said to have come *down to* man since he assumed our lowly human nature when "the Word was made flesh and dwelt among us" (John 1:14). And Jesus, *having seen, was moved with pity.* That is, having seen for the first time by experiential knowledge the condition of suffering humanity, he was moved in his Sacred Heart with pity for us. *And having come to him, he bound up his wounds.* For Jesus came *down to* us by the Incarnation, but he came *near to* us by accepting the defects of sinful flesh and by enduring suffering for our sakes, and in this way he bound up our wounds: "By his stripes we were healed" (Isa. 53:5).

And he provides a remedy by *pouring on oil and wine;* that is, by means of his mercy and justice. For wine disinfects the wounds while stinging the flesh. In the same way, divine justice counteracts the lure of creatures by which the love of them infects the soul, and it does this by stinging the flesh; that is, by withdrawing the pleasures of created goods and thereby revealing their inability to bring us happiness. Moreover, the sting of the wine makes us more acutely aware of our wounds, and in the same way divine justice makes us aware of our sins and misery, so that we might more readily confess them. On the other hand, oil both soothes the flesh and heals it. And so also divine mercy comforts us in our afflictions and heals us of our sins. For in every sin there is a twofold motion: the conversion to creatures and the aversion from God.

By divine justice, the conversion to creatures and the forgetfulness of God that it begets are remedied. By divine mercy, the aversion from God is remedied, for through this mercy we are reunited to God.

And having mounted him upon his own beast—that is, upon the humanity that he assumed for our salvation and in which he bore our sins—*brought him to an inn*. This inn signifies the Church, because the Church is a place of safety and healing in this life while we await the Lord's return. *And he took care of him*, since there he provided all those things necessary for man's salvation in superabundance. *And the next day*—that is, the day of the Resurrection—*he put out two denarii*. These two coins signify the keys of the Kingdom of Heaven (the sacrament of forgiveness of sins), by which what is bound on earth is bound in heaven and what is loosed on earth is loosed in heaven. *And he gave them to the innkeeper*; that is, to St. Peter and the apostles. And he said, *"Take care of him; and whatever you may spend over and above I will give back to you when I return*, namely at my Second Coming.

But how can it be that something is spent over and above what Christ had already been given? St. Paul tells us: "I make up in my own body what is lacking in the sufferings of Christ, for the sake of his body the Church" (Col. 1:24). Paul does not mean the sufferings of Christ were not sufficient; he means that Christ willed that the merits of his Passion be applied through the ministry of the saints so they might participate, as secondary causes, in his redemption and become true causes in their own right of the sanctification of the Church.

When we look back over this parable, we see the fall of mankind, the inability of the old law and priesthood to heal fallen mankind, the Incarnation and Passion, the foundation of the Church, the Resurrection and, finally, the Second Coming. The whole history of salvation is recounted here in summary fashion. This sheds a bright light on the literal sense of the parable. The reason anyone who needs mercy is our neighbor is that God became our neighbor to show mercy to us first. We did not have correct beliefs, but while we were still sinners God became man and dwelt among us and gave his life for us. If God can be our neighbor and we can be God's neighbor, then there is no person who is excluded from our compassion or works of mercy.

This is why the second commandment is like the first: because there is a proportion between God's love for us and our love for our neighbor: "Beloved, if God so loved us, we also must love one another" (1 John 4:11); "for whoever does not love a brother whom he has seen cannot love God whom he has not seen" (1 John 4:20).

Being Evangelized by the
Parable of the Good Samaritan

Each of us has been wounded by original sin. We have added to this wound by our own personal sins. But Jesus has drawn near to us in his compassion and bathed and bound up these wounds by baptism. He has entrusted us to his Church until he comes again. Therefore, it is in and with the Church that we will find healing and strength. By trusting the Church, we entrust ourselves to Jesus. Let us grow strong and be nourished by the bread of true doctrine and the healing balm of the sacrament of penance given to the whole Church through his innkeeper, the successor of St. Peter.

Evangelizing by Means of the
Parable of the Good Samaritan

The Samaritans were not just strangers, they were also considered heretics and enemies of the Jewish people. When they would not welcome Jesus as he was on his way to Jerusalem, John wanted to call down fire from heaven to destroy them, just as the prophet Elijah had done some centuries earlier (Luke 9:54; 2 Kings 1:10–14). But it was only a short time after Jesus' Ascension when John was sent not to call down destroying fire, but the saving fire of the Holy Spirit, because the Samaritans had received the word of God with such fervor (Acts 8:14–17). In the same way, we must look upon the enemies of the Church as objects of salvation and divine mercy. Indeed, many of them may become the most fervent converts to the Faith. After all, St. Paul was a converted Pharisee. Evangelization excludes no one.

CHAPTER 7

THE MAN BORN BLIND

This passage about the man born blind is, like the passage about the Samaritan woman at the well, found only in the Gospel of St. John. It is also read in the Church especially during Lent, and it is particularly instructive for those preparing for baptism.

As Jesus passed by he saw a man blind from birth. His disciples asked him: "Rabbi, who sinned, this man or his parents, that he was born blind?" Jesus answered, "Neither he nor his parents sinned; it is so that the works of God might be made visible through him. We have to do the works of the one who sent me while it is day. Night is coming when no one can work. While I am in the world, I am the light of the world." When he had said this, he spat on the ground and made clay with the saliva, and smeared the clay on his eyes, and said to him, "Go wash in the Pool of Siloam" (Siloam means Sent).

So he went and washed, and came back able to see. His neighbors and those who had seen him earlier as a beggar said, "Isn't this the one who used to sit and beg?" Some said, "It is," but others said, "No, he just looks like him."

He said, "I am." So they said to him, "How were your eyes opened?" He replied, "The man called Jesus made clay and anointed my eyes and told me, 'Go to Siloam and wash.' So I went there and washed and was able to see." And they said to him, "Where is he?" He said, "I don't know."

They brought the one who was once blind to the Pharisees. Now Jesus had made clay and opened his eyes on a Sabbath. So then the Pharisees also asked him how he was able to see. He said to them, "He put clay on my eyes, and I washed, and now I can see." So some of the Pharisees said, "This man is not from God, because he does not keep the Sabbath." But others said, "How can a sinful man do such signs?" And there was a division among them. So they said to the blind man again, "What do you have to say about him, since he opened your eyes?" He said, "He is a prophet."

Now the Jews did not believe that he had been blind and gained his sight until they summoned the parents of the one who had gained his sight. They asked them, "Is this your son, who you say was born blind? How does he now see?" His parents answered and said, "We know that this is our son and that he was born blind. We do not know how he sees now, nor do we know who opened his eyes. Ask him, he is of age; he can speak for himself." His parents said this because they were afraid of the Jews, for the Jews had already agreed that if anyone acknowledged him as the Messiah, he would be expelled from the synagogue. For this reason his parents said, "He is of age; question him."

So a second time they called the man who had been blind and said to him, "Give God the praise! We know that this man is a sinner." He replied, "If he is a sinner, I do not know. One thing I do know is that I was blind and now I see." So they said to him, "What did he do to you? How did he open your eyes?" He answered them, "I told you already and you did not listen. Why do you want to hear it again? Do you want to become his disciples, too?" They ridiculed him and said, "You are that man's disciple; we are disciples of Moses! We know that God spoke to Moses, but we do not know where this one is from."

The man answered and said to them, "This is what is so amazing, that you do not know where he is from, yet he opened my eyes. We know that God does not listen to sinners, but if one is devout and does his will, he listens to him. It is unheard of that anyone ever opened the eyes of a person born blind. If this man were not from God, he would not be able to do anything." They answered and said to him, "You were born totally in sin, and are you trying to teach us?" Then they threw him out.

When Jesus heard that they had thrown him out, he found him and said, "Do you believe in the Son of Man?" He answered and said, "Who is he, sir, that I may believe in him?" Jesus said to him, "You have seen him and the one speaking with you is he." He said, "I do believe, Lord," and he worshipped him. Then Jesus said, "I came into this world for judgment, so that those who do not see might see, and those who do see might become blind." Some of the Pharisees who were with him heard this and said to him, "Surely we are not also blind, are we?" Jesus said to them, "If you were blind, you would have no sin; but now you are saying, 'We see,' so your sin remains" (John 9:1–41).

Most of this passage is not a conversation between Jesus and the man born blind. Jesus appears only at the beginning and the end of this passage. Rather, it is mostly a record of the words of those who refuse to believe the testimony of the man born blind. To call their words a conversation would be a misnomer, since they really have no interest in listening to him or even addressing him. They are mostly talking to themselves. Jesus seems to be the only one who actually enters into a real conversation with the man born blind. This is already very instructive. It is possible to have a conversation without any real communication passing between the interlocutors.

The Context of the Conversation

The occasion for this account is that the disciples are wondering about the reason why someone could be blind from birth. They are operating on the premise that it must be a punishment, yet at the same time how could someone sin who was not yet born? So they immediately suspect the parents. The possibility of a sin that is passed on from the parents to their child at birth should remind Christians of the doctrine of original sin, a doctrine that will loom largely in the spiritual sense of the passage.

The Literal Sense

The passage begins with the words, *As Jesus passed by he saw a man blind from birth.* Jesus saw him, but he obviously did not see Jesus. And this is a theme throughout the passage: Jesus takes the initiative to enter into the life of someone who cannot take the initiative. What is more, the man born blind knows that he cannot take the initiative. As a careful reading of the passage will confirm, he is the epitome of the humble man, the one who knows he can do nothing without the help of others, whose only hope is in God. And yet it is this very humility that sounds more loudly in the ears of Jesus than the clamor of multitudes. Jesus seems to be drawn to him like iron to a magnet.

Right away the disciples ask Jesus about whose sin was the cause of his blindness from birth. On the one hand, it seems that someone should be punished for their own sins; therefore blindness must have been a punishment for his own sin. On the other hand, since he was blind from birth, it seems that he would not have had any opportunity to sin, so that his parents must be to blame. But Jesus responds by refuting their initial assumption: namely, that all physical evils are a punishment for sin. Rather, sometimes a physical evil is permitted by God to afflict even just men, such as holy Job, in order to bring about and manifest some greater good. And such was the present case. Jesus declares this man free from sin and reveals the real reason for his blindness: this man was born in darkness so that the light of God might shine upon the whole world.

Without further ado, Jesus performs a miracle: he gives sight to the man born blind. But the manner in which he effects the cure demands humility and obedience from the one who receives it. Jesus does not simply say, "Receive your sight." No, instead he does something that must have been very humiliating for the blind man. He makes mud from his spittle and smears this mud in his eyes. Notice, there is no initial promise of a cure, just mud in his eyes and on his face, and the command to go wash in the pool of Siloam. The blind man accepts all this without a word of protest, a sign of his great humility.

And then, just as Jesus tells him, he goes all the way to the pool of Siloam to wash. The pool of Siloam was all the way across the city, so for a blind man to walk that entire distance with mud in his eyes and on his face was a significant hardship. If he had not believed, he certainly would have washed somewhere closer. Moreover, it was the Sabbath, a day on which long journeys were prohibited. But this man, who was in the darkness of his blindness, was illumined interiorly by the light of faith. How great is the faith of one who believes that what has never been wrought by any prophet in any age should be accomplished by the one who sent him. His humility was profound, his obedience prompt, his faith perfect. And so he goes, he washes, he sees.

Immediately a controversy breaks out about this man. Those who knew him previously begin to debate among themselves about whether this was the same man who used to be a blind beggar. Notice, they do not even bother asking him, treating him as unworthy of their conversation. They do not consider him to be a fit witness of his own identity, so little regard did they have for him! Because he had been healed on the Sabbath, and this miracle seemed to involve a violation of the Sabbath, the Pharisees get involved. They too begin to dispute among themselves, not bothering to speak with him first. And when he asserts that Jesus did in fact cure him of blindness, they refuse to believe him and call in his parents as witnesses. Once again, they disdain him so greatly that they do not consider him to be a fit witness of his own identity.

Finally, forced to admit that a miracle has indeed taken place, they call him in again and try to get him to testify that Jesus is a sinner. They assert something that they do not know: *We know this man is a sinner,* they say. They say they see something that they do not see, and so they are more blind than this man had been before Jesus healed him. He responds by placing the facts before them again: *One thing I do know is that I was blind and now I see.* They react to this obvious truth by manifesting that they are deaf as well. For they ask him again the same question they asked him before, as if they had never heard his first answer: *I told you already and you did not listen. Why do you want to hear it again?* The man born blind is without guile, and he does not attribute evil motives to them; he asks in all innocence: Do you want to become his disciples too? At this point, he confesses that he is a disciple of Jesus: one who has eyes to see and ears to hear the word of Christ.

At this, the Pharisees react violently, ridiculing him and berating him. They pretend to be disciples of Moses, even though they have not understood what Moses wrote. But this uneducated man refutes their claim with an argument framed in impeccable logic: *This is what is so amazing, that you do not know where he is from, yet he opened my eyes. We know that God does not listen to sinners, but if one is devout and does his will, he listens to him. It is unheard of that anyone ever opened the eyes of a person born blind. If this man were not from God, he would not be able to do anything.*

It is very interesting that he knew that, from the beginning of the world, never had one born blind been cured. We can imagine that as a child he had heard about the curing of diseases by the prophets of old, and he asked his parents if anyone born blind had ever been cured. How disappointed he must have felt when they told him that it had never happened. The fact itself is strange. The prophets of old had performed many remarkable miracles: the dividing of the Red Sea, calling down fire from heaven, the curing of lepers, even raising the dead. Why had it never been known that the eyes of one born blind were opened? This curious fact will serve as a key for unlocking the spiritual sense of this passage.

They cannot refute his argument, so instead they attempt to assassinate his character by asserting something else they could not know: *You were born totally in sin, and are you trying to teach us?* Before they had accused Jesus of sin, now they accuse this man of sin: a man whom the Creator himself declared free from sin. If he were so ignorant due to his sin, it would have been an easy thing to refute his argument. But this they could not do, for he spoke truthfully. Instead they cast him out, forbidding him access to the synagogue and to the temple, the only place of worship he had ever known—the one place where, from his youth, he had learned how to love God. And so there he sat, poor, alone, and discarded, forbidden to worship the God he loved in the only place he knew how to worship him.

He has suffered persecution and great sorrow for the love of Jesus, but now he does not know where to look for him. But behold, just when he is seeking God in his heart without knowing how to find him, he is sought and found by his God: *When Jesus heard that they had thrown him out, he found him.* The intensity of his longing and humility draw Jesus to himself, just as the longing tears of Mary Magdalene would later draw Jesus to her at the tomb. Finding him outside the place of worship, Jesus asks for an act of worship: a profession of faith. For the Father seeks those who will worship him in spirit and truth. Jesus asks: *Do you believe in the Son of Man?* In his humility he simply acknowledges his need for a teacher, saying: *Who is he, sir, that I may believe in him?* Jesus said to him, *You have seen him and the one speaking with you is he.*

With what love and tenderness Jesus must have said these words, and how they must have resonated in the heart of this little man who, finally, for once in his life, has found someone who loves him. And the one who loves him is the one whom he had always loved but did not yet know. It is I, the incarnate Word of God, who speaks with you. Though father and mother abandon you the Lord has received you (Ps. 27:10). Though men disdain your conversation, I, your God, desire it. Though men consider you unfit for worship, your Creator declares you fit: *He said, "I do believe, Lord"* (as if to say, *Credo in unum Deum*) *and he worshipped him.* Such is the fate of the humble: God himself finds them irresistible;

they are sought as the companions of God. He seeks them out and fills them with his graces, at last bestowing upon them the vision of his face that they might love him and know that they are loved by him. How good God is to the humble soul.

There are a number of striking likenesses between the man born blind and the Samaritan woman at the well: (1) both do not recognize him at first; (2) Jesus takes the initiative with both; (3) both are seeking water; (4) both regard him as a prophet after their initial encounter with him; (5) both tell others about Jesus so that they might become his disciples too; (6) both wonder about where they might worship God; (7) both are asked to make a profession of faith in Jesus as the Son of God; and (8) both are considered unworthy of the conversation of men, yet are sought out for conversation with God. The Holy Spirit obviously intends for us to compare the two.

The Spiritual Sense

We have so far considered the literal sense of the passage about the man born blind but, not surprisingly, there is a profound spiritual sense to this passage as well. *As Jesus passed by, he saw a man who was blind from birth.* In the scriptures bodily things are signs of spiritual realities. And so blindness is often the outward sign of interior sinfulness. For example, the book of Wisdom says, "their wickedness blinded them" (2:21); the first letter of John says, "Whoever hates his brother is in darkness; he walks in darkness and does not know where he is going because the darkness has blinded his eyes" (2:11). This is why the disciples immediately ask about sin when they see that the man is blind.

What could blindness from birth signify? Sin from birth, or *original sin* as it has come to be known. In light of this, let us reread the opening verse: *As Jesus passed by, he saw a man who was blind from birth.* That is, as Jesus was passing through this world on his way back to his Father, he saw mankind subject to original sin. And while he was still in the world as its light, it was time to effect a cure for original sin. In fact, the connection between original sin and blindness was so deeply ingrained in the consciousness of the first Christians that they used to call baptism "illumination." And St. Augustine once said that on account of the sin of Adam that has infected our nature, every man is spiritually born blind. Once we understand this meaning, the entire passage falls into place. For example, the question about his parent's sin makes perfect sense.

Let us return to that curious fact we noticed above. Why was it that from the foundation of the world, never had it been heard that someone opened the eyes of one born blind? The reason no prophet had ever been able to heal a man born blind is that no prophet had arisen who had the power to heal the wound of original sin that blindness from birth signified. For every prophet suffered from that same wound of our common human nature.

Therefore, it was only when Jesus came that the wound of original sin could be healed. For only he who created our nature could recreate it. Finally, there was something new under the sun. And see how the divine physician heals: by making mud from the earth and applying it to his eyes. Human nature was made by God in the beginning from the mud of the earth (Gen. 2:7), so Jesus uses mud to perform this miracle to signify both that he was the God who first formed man from mud, and that he has come to restore human nature to its original condition.

The man is commanded by Jesus to go wash in the pool of Siloam, but this pool was far away and therefore the man had to make a long journey without yet being able to see. This journey signifies the long night of faith through which we must pass in this world until we see God face-to-face in the next. The washing in the pool signifies baptism, by which we are spiritually illumined, and the eyes of our soul are opened to divine truth through faith. It is also interesting that some ancient authors record that the pool of Siloam was fed by a spring called the Spring of the Virgin. This would imply the teaching that all grace, even sacramental grace such as the grace of baptism, flows through and from the Virgin Mary. So this miracle can be understood in its spiritual sense to signify the institution of the sacrament of baptism.

Being Evangelized by the Conversation with the Man Born Blind

If we have humility, Christ will find us. We do not even need to look for him. It is therefore of utmost importance that we prize and cultivate this attitude of humility before all others. Humility is not self-hatred. Rather, it is the awareness of radical dependence upon the love and mercy of your Father in heaven: it involves a sense of being a child at the core of your being. The infant being held in its Father's arms does not experience self-hatred; he experiences being nothing except an object of love; he is an emptiness being constantly filled by the love of a Father. The humble man is not only aware that God has given him the commandment to love him with all our being, but he is also aware that God has given a commandment to himself to love us with all his being. It is as if God says to us: "You don't have to worry about loving yourself anymore: that's my job. You just focus on loving me, and I will focus on loving you." The emptiness of humility is an emptying of self-love, not the emptiness of self-hatred.

There will be times, of course, when you cannot see where God is leading you. That is okay. There will even be times when you get mud in your face and eyes. Continue to walk trustingly and believe what you hear. Do not demand to see for yourself: "We walk by faith, not by sight" (2 Cor. 5:7). If we allow ourselves to be led in this way, truly the glory of God will be revealed in us.

Evangelizing by Means of the Conversation with the Man Born Blind

True humility, far from making us shy and afraid to speak to others of Christ's love, emboldens us. We should never be afraid to speak to others about the miracles Christ has done in us. And even if others treat us with disdain, we should say with the blind man: "Do you also want to become his disciple?"

Sometimes the people to whom we speak will claim to know that they have the sure means of salvation, even though they do not know Christ. They are like those who claim to be disciples of Moses, but not of Jesus about whom Moses wrote (see John 5:46). In fact, it is not Moses they need to abandon, but their wrong understanding of him. In other words, they need not abandon the legitimate means of salvation to which they cling, but rather they need to understand it as pointing to Jesus Christ. Evangelization always points to Christ and the means of salvation he has established, yet it preserves all that is good and holy in the lives of those to whom we are sent.

CHAPTER 8

THE PARALYTIC MAN

The next conversation I want to reflect on is the passage about the healing of the paralytic man. This conversation teaches us much about the importance of friends in our spiritual life, and it has a special significance for priests.

And it came to pass on a certain day, as he sat teaching, that there were also Pharisees and doctors of the law sitting by that were come out of every town of Galilee, and Judea, and Jerusalem. And the power of the Lord was to heal them. And behold, men brought in a bed a man who had the palsy. And they sought means to bring him in, and to lay him before him. And when they could not find by what way they might bring him in, because of the multitude, they went up upon the roof, and let him down through the tiles with his bed in the midst before Jesus. Whose faith, when he saw, he said, "Man, your sins are forgiven you."

And the scribes and the Pharisees began to think, saying: "Who is this who speaks blasphemies. Who can forgive sins but God alone?" And when Jesus knew their thoughts, answering he said to them: "What is it you think in your hearts? That is easier to say: your sins are forgiven you; or to say, arise and walk? But so that you may know that the Son of Man has the power on earth to forgive sins (he says to the one sick with the palsy), I say to you: Arise, take up your bed and go into your house." And immediately rising up before them, he took up his bed on which he lay and went away to his own house glorifying God. And all were astonished, and they glorified God. And they were filled with fear saying: "We have seen wonderful things today" (Luke 5:17–26).

The Context of the Conversation

Throughout the fourth and fifth chapters of St. Luke's Gospel, Jesus is traveling around and teaching. Significantly, in the fifth chapter, he is teaching outside of the synagogues, which was a kind of innovation. Jesus is going outside of the customary context for teaching and preaching. Jesus was bringing to the people a new revelation, the gospel, and they needed to be prepared to receive it. This included not only the people and his disciples, but also the leaders of the Jewish people. It is precisely these latter whom Jesus is trying to heal in this conversation: "There were also Pharisees and doctors of the law sitting by that were come out of every town of Galilee, and Judea, and Jerusalem. And the power of the Lord was to heal *them*."

The Literal Sense

Among the many beautiful truths revealed in this passage is the truth that sometimes we need friends for our salvation. When the men bring the paralytic before Jesus, we are told that Jesus saw *their* faith, the faith of his friends, and as a result forgave the sins of the paralyzed man. Sometimes we are in such a state of spiritual paralysis that we are not even capable of bringing ourselves before the Lord, of even asking for forgiveness. It is times like these that we need true friends who can bring us before the Lord, who can make the sacrifices necessary to carry us; as St. Paul says, "Bear you one another's burdens" (Gal. 6:2). So often in the scriptures, Jesus heals someone physically or spiritually, or both, because of the prayers, the sacrifices, the efforts of someone who loves him, of a friend. This communion of saints interceding for one another is God's will, and he even permits us to be real instruments in communicating his greatest gifts—even the gift of forgiveness of sins, of salvation itself.

A second truth revealed in this passage, not unrelated to the first, is that God can communicate to human nature the power to forgive sins, and he has done so. Look carefully back at the passage. The Pharisees object to Jesus claiming the power to forgive sins: *Who can forgive sins but God alone?* Once, a friend of mine gave me an article written in a newsletter by a former Catholic seminarian who decided to become a Presbyterian minister. He said that he could not go on with his studies for the priesthood since Catholic priests claim the power to forgive sins, but that the scriptures say, "Who can forgive sins but God alone?" In his article, he failed to mention that those words were the words of the Pharisees charging Jesus with blasphemy. So I wrote this fellow and pointed this out.

He responded by saying that the whole point of the passage was to show that Jesus was God. True enough, I replied. But if that were the only point at stake, then we would expect Jesus to say something like this to the Pharisees and scribes: "Well, it turns out that I am God, so that's why I can forgive sins." But Jesus does not answer that way; instead he specifically points to his human nature when claiming the power to forgive sins. He says, *So that you may know that the Son of Man has the power on earth to forgive sins . . .* and then performs a miracle to manifest that it is through his humanity that he forgave this man's sins. He does not say, "So that you may know the Son of God has the power in heaven to forgive sins," or "So that you may know I am the Son of God," but rather insists that the forgiveness of sins is something he does as the Son of Man on earth. In the parallel passage in the Gospel of St. Matthew, it even says that the people glorified God that he had "given such power to men," and the only mention of power before that in the passage was the power to forgive sins.

Now the fact that Jesus is forgiving sins through his human nature becomes very significant. For if he can communicate that power to his own human nature, he can also communicate it to ours. And that is exactly what we see him doing after the Resurrection: "Receive the Holy Spirit: whose sins you shall forgive, they are forgiven them" (John 2:22–23). First Jesus communicates a special share of the divine nature to his priests by giving them the Holy Spirit; then, as a consequence of sharing in the divine nature, they receive the power to forgive sins as human instruments of the Holy Spirit. So not only is it true that we need friends for our salvation, to have our sins forgiven, but it is also true that the priest is the great friend of the soul, since he has received from God the power to forgive sins in his name.

The Spiritual Sense

We can see the profound spiritual sense of this passage as well. For the man with the palsy represents the soul in bondage to sin, for one who sins is no longer the master of his own actions, but is, so to speak, held fast by his sin. And he is brought to the Lord by men (i.e., the priests) in a bed (i.e., his body). And not finding a way to lay him before Jesus because of the multitudes (i.e., the multitude of this world's cares), they brought him up to the rooftop (i.e., to the heights of contemplation through prayer). For the priest intercedes on behalf of sinful mankind through the act of contemplative worship.

After that, they let him down through the tiles. These tiles signify the sacraments of the Church. For the tiles are material things placed up high, so they aptly signify the sacraments that are material things put to the most noble use. And the man is said to be lowered through them since he is humbled by subjecting himself to the sacramental order. As St. Thomas says, "Man is brought low [through the sacraments], since he recognizes himself to be subject to corporeal things, while help is brought to him through corporeal things."[27] Then he is laid in the midst—that is, in the assembly of the saints and angels—before Jesus. Jesus first forgives his sins, and then commands him to rise, take up his bed, and go to his home. And this signifies the final resurrection, when, at the voice of the Lord, all the dead shall rise, take up their bodies now made incorruptible, and enter into their eternal home.

Some Reflections on the Difference Between Catholic and Protestant Theology

The revelation that God uses the instrument of human nature and even of bodily things to forgive sins opens up a larger question: why does God want to use human or created instruments at all? Why doesn't he just do everything directly? I think this principle—namely, that God wills to use created instruments to bring about the salvation of souls—is the fundamental difference between Catholics and Protestants.

Years ago, when I was a student at Thomas Aquinas College in California, a young man who was a very serious Protestant started as a freshman there. His case was unusual to say the least. He was already married with four small children. He had been a nominal Catholic until college, when he left the practice of his faith to become a member of a very devout Protestant group. In fact, he wanted to become a Protestant minister, so he decided to go to a top-notch Catholic college where he could learn all the best Catholic arguments in order to refute them. But with all that, he was an honest man, not someone with an axe to grind, and he was willing to listen to a reasonable argument.

His first semester he was looking for a house for his family to move into. His saintly and uber-competent wife took care of the kids while he lived temporarily in the dorms. There, he and I would get into knock-down, drag-out arguments about everything Catholic and Protestant (I had been a convert myself). We often stayed up till two or three in the morning. And on one occasion he made this objection: "My mother has all these pictures of Mary around the house, and only a couple of Jesus. That's just completely wrong. It's like Mary is more important than Jesus. What could Mary possibly have that Jesus doesn't? Why would anyone pray to Mary, or any saint for that matter?"

I don't remember exactly how I answered him on that occasion, besides telling him that I liked his mother very much, and she sounded like a very good Catholic (I would always be on the offensive for those things: Catholics are always apologizing for things they shouldn't be apologizing about). But I know what I would say now if asked that question.

Jesus once said, "He that believes in me will do the works that I do, and greater than these shall he do" (John 14:12). That is a remarkable statement, and it came true. For example, Jesus never healed anyone with his shadow, but Peter did (Acts 5:15). Jesus never converted 3,000 persons in one sermon, but Peter did (Acts 2:41). Some saints performed more remarkable resurrections than Jesus did. For example, St. Vincent Ferrer raised a child that had been totally dismembered. Why is it that some saints performed greater miracles than Jesus did? Is it because Jesus could not do this himself? Clearly not. But for some reason, Jesus wanted to do more through Peter and his other disciples than directly himself. I can think of at least five reasons why God would choose to do greater works through the instrumentality of his saints than directly.

First, every father has the experience of wanting his children to be as good as they can be. In fact, I know of no father who does not desire that his children be better than himself. God is no exception. He wants to communicate as much good as possible to his children, and he wants them to have and be worthy of as much honor as possible. So God communicates the dignity of being true and real causes of salvation to his children. This makes his creatures more like himself.

Second, God uses creatures as his instruments in accomplishing his work in order to manifest his own power and wisdom. Take this simple example. Two artists each paint a painting. The first one has perfect instruments: an assortment of perfect brushes, perfect canvas, all the right colors, and so on. And so he paints a masterpiece. The second artist has one lousy brush, a bad canvas, and just a few primary colors. Yet he paints the same masterpiece. Who is the greater artist? Clearly the second artist is, since by painting the same masterpiece, but with defective instruments, he manifests the perfection of his ability as an artist. God likes to use defective instruments in order to show off his ability and his wisdom as an artist. St. Paul says as much when he asserts:

Not many of you were wise by human standards, not many were powerful, not many were of noble birth. Rather, God chose the foolish of the world to shame the wise, and God chose the weak of the world to shame the strong, and God chose the lowly and despised of the world, those who count for nothing, to reduce to nothing those who are something, so that no human being might boast before God (1 Cor. 1:26–29).

Again, Paul asserts the same principle when he says, "The Lord said, 'My grace is sufficient for you, for power is made perfect in weakness.' I will rather boast most gladly of my weaknesses, in order that the power of Christ may dwell with me" (2 Cor. 12:9). Once, St. Bernadette of Lourdes testified that if the Blessed Mother had found "a more ignorant and stupid child on earth," she would have chosen her; but she couldn't find one, so she chose St. Bernadette.[28]

A third reason God wants to use creatures in order to communicate his goodness to us is that it puts us at ease. In the Old Testament, God appeared in a theophany on Mount Sinai. There he showed his majesty and power, but the result was not love but fear and terror in the hearts of the Israelites:

When the people witnessed the thunder and lightning, the trumpet blast and the mountain smoking, they all feared and trembled. So they took up a position much farther away and said to Moses, "You speak to us, and we will listen; but let not God speak to us, or we shall die." Moses answered the people: "Do not be afraid, for God has come to you only to test you and put his fear upon you, lest you should sin." Still the people remained at a distance (Exod. 20:19–21).

God, like any father, does not want his children to remain at a distance, so he uses mediators to set us at ease. The people were able to somehow communicate with God through Moses. Later on, God would himself become man and use the created instrument of his sacred humanity to set us at ease, coming in the form of a baby, and later under the form of bread. For who could be frightened of a little child or a piece of bread? God did this knowing full well that familiarity breeds contempt, but he was willing to allow himself to be treated by us with contempt for the sake of having us draw closer to him. The humility of God is unfathomable. Often too, we feel afraid to approach Christ directly, but when we think of his mother or one of the saints who are mere men like us, we are set at ease. This is what the Lord himself prophecies in the prophet Hosea: "I will draw them with the cords of Adam, with the bands of love" (Hos. 11:4).

Related to this third reason is a fourth reason God prefers to use his saints as instruments to communicate grace: namely, so that we can see more easily how we ought to love God in the concrete circumstances of our lives. When Jesus walked this earth, he walked it at a certain time and place, in certain concrete circumstances sometimes very different from our own. The facile question, "What would Jesus do?" does not always give us a clear indication of how we ought to act in the here and now. Jesus was a man. How can a woman relate to everything he did? Jesus was a first-century Jew from Palestine. How can a twenty-first-century American imitate him in every respect? Most importantly, Jesus was God, so there are some things he did and said that we just can't imitate.

Every saint, being an instrument of the Holy Spirit, lived out the gospel in the concrete circumstances of his life in a perfect or near perfect way. Each one is like a perfect living out of the commandments incarnated in a new time and place and circumstances, closer to our own. This makes it much easier to know how to act. Some saints were scholars, like St. Thomas Aquinas; some were jovial, like St. Philip Neri, some were diocesan priests, like St. John Vianney; some were laymen, like St. Pier Giorgio Frassati; some were nuns, like St. Teresa of

Avila; some were wives and mothers, like St. Monica; and so on. Each gives us a more concrete example of how to follow Christ in our particular vocations and circumstances. Besides this, if I am looking for an example of repentance, it will be hard to follow Jesus' life, since he never had to repent. But it will be much easier to follow St. Peter or St. Mary Magdalene. Thus, we read in the scriptures that not only should we imitate Christ, but also his saints: "We wanted to present ourselves as a model for you, so that you might imitate us" (2 Thess. 3:9).

The fifth and perhaps most profound reason why God should choose human instruments to communicate his grace and salvation to us is in order to strengthen the bonds of love between men. If God truly uses us as instruments of his grace and salvation, if he uses the person who baptized you to give you the divine life, or the priest who absolved your sins to put you in his grace, or the friend who prayed and obtained the grace for your conversion, or whatever, then we shall have them to thank one day for a good as great as salvation itself. When all is said and done, and we are safely in our fatherland, we shall be able to look one another in the eye and say: "Thank you. If it had not been for you, I would not have been saved." And this will increase our love for one another in heaven tremendously. Nor will we love God any less, since we will see clearly that all grace and salvation has its original source in God, even though it came to us through instruments, like the fruit from the vine through the branches. So it's a win–win scenario for God if he uses us as his instruments: we will not love God any less, but we will love one another much more. And isn't this what a father most of all desires for his children, that they love one another as much as possible?

I don't think that a theology that denies that God generally prefers to use instruments to cause grace and salvation can stand in the face of revelation or of reason. The kind of theology that denies that God uses instruments as true causes is really the result of a nominalist philosophy that denies universal or secondary causes. God wants to encourage us to go to him through his saints. And to do this, he more quickly and readily answers our prayers and gives us greater gifts if we come to him through them: "They shall do greater works than I." That's why I'm okay with the pious Catholic mother having more images of the Blessed Virgin Mary than of Jesus. It's not because she loves Mary more than Jesus. It's because she has confidence that God wants to give her more if she comes to him with and through Mary.

By the way, that young man I told you about eventually gave up his plans to become a Protestant minister. He came back to the Church, and now has eleven beautiful children. He was even selected by his classmates to be the valedictorian. He spent most of his talk encouraging devotion to the Blessed Mother.

Being Evangelized by the Conversation with the Paralytic

Jesus wills to heal and sanctify us through his chosen instruments: through our family and friends, through the sacraments, through the priesthood. This can be humiliating. It is easy to submit ourselves to the all-powerful, all-knowing, all-holy God. It is easy to ask forgiveness and help directly from God. But to entrust our salvation to defective creatures who are often weak, ignorant, and sinful can be humiliating. Yet God's power shines through weakness: "the weakness of God is stronger than human strength" (1 Cor. 1:25). It is essential for our own conversion that we accept and humbly submit to God's plan for our sanctification and salvation. And His plan for our salvation is not "God alone can forgive sins" but rather God through Jesus Christ and his Church.

Evangelizing by Means of the
Conversation with the Paralytic

This conversation is an excellent starting point for evangelizing those who believe in God, and even in Jesus, but who do not yet believe in his Church. Yet, the Apostle's Creed clearly states that we believe in the Church and the communion of saints. It is helpful to read the passage together and then ask: What role do the paralytic's friends play in the forgiveness of his sins? Why does Jesus contradict the Pharisees who say only God can forgive sins? Sometimes people are afraid that if someone or something other than God is introduced as an instrument or mediator of grace, then it will fail, and they will be lost.

The Pharisees thought this about Jesus himself. If forgiveness of sins comes through a man, how can we be certain of salvation? To accept God's wise and provident plan to make use of defective creatures to accomplish his purpose for our salvation demands great trust, great faith. Jesus said this same thing to his own disciples when he said, "Do not let your hearts be troubled. You have faith in God; have faith also in me" (John 14:1).

To have faith even in the defective instruments God has ordained for our salvation is to trust that God is in complete control of absolutely everything, even the most fallible of creatures. It is to believe that "all things work for good for those who love God" (Rom. 8:28). God can unfailingly bring about our salvation even through failing creatures. Now that is the kind of trust that God can work with.

CHAPTER 9

Jairus and the Woman with a Hemorrhage

St. Luke records the encounter between Jesus, Jairus, and the woman with a hemorrhage. The passage seems at first to be an intertwining of two unrelated events. Jairus comes to Jesus looking for a cure for his daughter. On the way, a woman with a hemorrhage stops him, she is healed, and then Jesus continues on his journey to raise the daughter of Jairus who has, in the meantime, died. The two events (the healing of the woman and the raising of the daughter) seem unrelated. But careful attention to the details of the story preclude such a superficial reading.

And it came to pass, that when Jesus returned, the multitude received him: for they were all waiting for him. And behold there came a man whose name was Jairus, and he was a ruler of the synagogue: and he fell down at the feet of Jesus, beseeching him that he would come into his house: For he had an only daughter, almost twelve years old, and she was dying. And it happened as he went, that he was thronged by the multitudes. And there was a certain woman having an issue of blood twelve years, who had bestowed all her substance on physicians, and could not be healed by any. She came behind him, and touched the hem of his garment; and immediately the issue of her blood stopped. And Jesus said, "Who is it that touched me?"

And all denying, Peter and they that were with him said, "Master, the multitudes throng and press you, and you say, 'Who touched me?'" And Jesus said, "Somebody has touched me; for I know that power is gone out from me." And the woman seeing that she was not hid, came trembling, and fell down before his feet, and declared before all the people for what cause she had touched him, and how she was immediately healed. But he said to her, "Daughter, your faith hath made you whole; go your way in peace."

As he was yet speaking, there came one to the ruler of the synagogue, saying to him, "Your daughter is dead, trouble him not." And Jesus hearing this word, answered the father of the maid, "Fear not; believe only, and she shall be safe." And when he was come to the house, he suffered not any man to go in with him, but Peter and James and John, and the father and mother of the maiden. And all wept and mourned for her. But he said, "Weep not; the maid is not dead, but sleeps." And they laughed him to scorn, knowing that she was dead. But he taking her by the hand, cried out, saying, "Maid, arise." And her spirit returned, and she arose immediately. And he bid them give her to eat. And her parents were astonished, whom he charged to tell no man what was done (Luke 8:40–56).

The Context of the Conversation

This conversation takes place in the eighth chapter of Luke's Gospel, and the person of Jairus bears some striking similarities with the centurion of the previous chapter (chapter seven). Both come to Jesus seeking the cure of a dying child. Both are rulers. The centurion has built a synagogue; Jairus is the ruler of a synagogue. So Jairus seems to be compared and even contrasted with the centurion. Whereas the centurion has perfect faith, and so does not need Jesus to come to his home, Jairus has a weak faith, and so needs Jesus to come to his home. Right away we find something instructive here. The weakness of Jairus's faith increases his own suffering. Had his faith been perfect like that of the centurion, there would have been no long and anxious journey back to his home, and his daughter would not have died while they were on the way.

Our own defects in faith end up adding unnecessarily to our sufferings in life. Often, Jesus wants to solve our problems right away, and he wants us to have confidence that they are solved as soon as we ask him (even when we can't see yet that they are solved) so that we can go about our lives in peace and joy. But we are the ones who limit his goodness: we insist on seeing the results we want right now; we insist on feeling Jesus' constant presence along the way; and consequently we pay the price. Something similar happens with the woman with a hemorrhage: she comes to Jesus after going to the doctors. By delaying, she seems to add to her own sufferings.

A story in which I was personally involved will help to illustrate the importance of trust in Jesus' care for us and our loved ones. Some years ago, a friend of mine whom I had known since we were teenagers told me that her grandmother (who was then 100 years old) was starting to fade, and she asked me if I could come visit her and talk to her about the Catholic faith. Her grandmother had been quite anti-Catholic for most of her life, but my friend, who had become Catholic in her youth, was hopeful that her grandmother would be more open as she approached death. I went to see her, and after a short conversation, she agreed to be baptized. At her baptism, she told her granddaughter something that greatly surprised her. She said, "My mother would be so happy!" My friend replied, "But grandma, you've been anti-Catholic your whole life. Why would your mother be so happy?"

"I never told you this," she responded, "but though my father was a staunch atheist, my mother had been Catholic and she was forbidden to have me baptized or raised in the Faith."

Here was the daughter of that forlorn Catholic mother being baptized more than a hundred years after she was born, and decades after her own mother died. And that's not all. Each of her direct descendants ended up Catholic too! My friend's mother was baptized on her deathbed; my friend, of course had converted on her own, and even her brother, who lived a wayward life, personally asked me to baptize him shortly before he died (he told me at the time that he wanted a "real Catholic funeral").

This poor woman had no hope of having her children raised Catholic, yet Jesus arranged that all her descendants came to the Church before they died. That story should give hope to all those parents who anguish over the salvation of their children. You may not live to see it, but Jesus loves your children more than you do, and he wants us to trust in his love, not to be anxious or afraid.

The Literal Sense

As I said before, this passage seems at first to be an intertwining of two unrelated events. But we must read the passage carefully, noting the various details if we want to understand the relationship between these two events. They say the devil is in the details, but in Scripture it is better to say that the Spirit is in the details!

The first detail is the coincidence that Jairus's daughter was twelve years old, while for the same length of time, twelve years, the woman had been suffering from a flow of blood. A mere coincidence? Perhaps. But consider this: in the same moment that Jesus says to the woman, *Daughter, your faith has made you whole*, Jairus receives the news that his daughter has died. Read the passage again: *[Jesus] said to her: Daughter, your faith hath made you whole; go your way in peace. As he was yet speaking, there came one to the ruler of the synagogue, saying to him: Your daughter is dead, trouble him not.* It mentions that the news of his daughter's death came simultaneously with Jesus' words to the woman. If you had been present at the scene, you would have heard it like this: "Daughter your faith has made you whole . . . your daughter is dead."

It is the only time in all the Gospels that Jesus calls someone his daughter. Why here? Why now? In order to call Jairus's attention to the fact that he was not the only person there who had a daughter in need of healing. Twelve years before, this woman began to hemorrhage. As a result, the woman would have been made ritually unclean by her flow of blood, and therefore would certainly have been excluded from participating in the worship at the synagogue where Jairus was an official, lest she contaminate anyone who had the duty of sacred worship. Indeed, it seems likely that it was Jairus himself who excluded her from the worship at the synagogue, since he was the ruler there. For twelve years this woman was excluded from the house of her Father, while for twelve years Jairus enjoyed the company of his own daughter in his house.

If this was indeed the case, we can wonder whether Jairus ever thought about this woman, whether he noticed her or remembered that she was excluded from God's house. Perhaps he did not even give her a second thought all these years.

But now, at the moment when his daughter lay desperately ill, when time was of the essence to heal her, this same woman delays Jesus from coming to his home. And it is certain now that he notices her. What was going on in his heart at this moment? Was he angry at her for holding Jesus up? Did he want her to just go away? All those thoughts came crashing down in the moment when he heard Jesus call her his daughter, and then in the next moment hear his servant say: "Do not trouble the master: your daughter is dead." By causing Jairus to reflect on the condition of his own daughter, and upon the pain he now felt at being separated from her, Jesus willed to arouse in Jairus a new sense of compassion for this woman whom he had not recognized as God's daughter.

This is instructive for us as well, since in our prayers we often ask from God the thing that we deny to others. And it is only when we recognize this fact that God will hear and answer our prayers. St. Peter Chrysologus once wrote: "When you fast, see the fasting of others. If you want God to know that you are hungry, know that another is hungry. If you hope for mercy, show mercy. If you look for kindness, show kindness. If you want to receive, give. If you ask for yourself what you deny to others, your asking is a mockery."[29] How often do we ask from God the things we deny to others? We ask for our daily bread, but we do not share our bread daily with the hungry. We ask for health, but we do not comfort the sick. We ask for friendship, but we do not offer friendship. We ask for forgiveness, but we refuse to forgive others. Mercy is at the heart of the New Law, and blessed are the merciful, for they shall receive mercy.

There is another interesting detail about the cure of the woman with a hemorrhage: when she touches Jesus, she is one of a multitude to touch him. They are pressing upon him while she barely touches the *hem of his garment*, yet she alone is healed. So often we come to Jesus in the same way that this multitude does. We throng, we press upon him, but we never truly touch him, because we do not come with faith, but rather with demands.

We would do well to meditate on what caused Jairus and the woman with a hemorrhage to respond to Jesus and the gospel in an imperfect way in contrast with the centurion who has perfect faith. What do Jairus and the woman with the hemorrhage have in common? First, they are afraid. They are afraid that Jesus can't help them, or if he can that he doesn't care enough about them to help. They let their fear prevent them from coming to Jesus with simplicity and trust. We can be the same way: we can sneak up behind Jesus because we don't think he loves us enough to want to help us if we just come to him directly and with confidence despite our sinfulness and misery.

The second thing they have in common is that they all seem to have some reason why they can trust in their own merits. Unlike the centurion, Jairus is a member of the Jewish people, and even a ruler of the synagogue; the woman is someone of substance who apparently started out with a lot of money that she ended up spending on doctors. They had something to hang their hat on other than the mercy of Christ. And so for them Jesus was not their first but their last resort.

To the degree that we rely upon our own talents, natural gifts, worldly wealth, or status, to the same extent will we put Jesus last and end up resisting the seed of the word that Christ wants to plant and bear fruit in our hearts. And yet in the face of all this, we should take some consolation in this fact: that in spite of their imperfections, Jesus does eventually give them what they need. He is so good that he grants our prayers even when we make them in the wrong way;

he loves us so much that he gives us more than we ask even when we make him our last resort!

Three Resurrection Miracles

The raising of Jairus's daughter is one of the three times the evangelists record that Jesus raised someone else from the dead. The other two are the raising of the son of the widow of Nain (Luke 7) and the raising of Lazarus, the brother of Mary and Martha (John 11). Notice that in each case Jesus raises someone from the dead at the prayers of a family member. And all the relationships within an immediate family are represented: father/daughter; mother/son; brother/sister. Even Jesus' own Resurrection seems to be in answer to the faith and prayer of his own mother, Mary, as the story of the widow of Nain implies.

This brings us back to the point I made in the last chapter: we need friends to pray for us; and the prayers of a family member are especially powerful. All of us have family members who are dead, either physically or spiritually. We must have confidence that Jesus wants to use our faith and prayers and tears as his instruments to raise up our dead family members from purgatory or from sin.

Sometimes a mother comes to me in despair because her son has died of a drug overdose, or in a sudden accident, seemingly unrepentant. At such times I remind her that Jesus can raise the dead, and that he can use her prayers to save her child. Nothing escapes his power, and all times—past, present and future—are present to his knowledge and grace. I tell her to trust like the centurion who did not need to see results right away, but rather to make her journey home to heaven in complete confidence and faith that Jesus will save her child. Sometimes parents or siblings come to me because their child or brother or sister is spiritually dead and away from the Church. I assure them that their prayers have a special power before Jesus to raise up their family member. We must pray trustingly and perseveringly, without fear or anxiety. God will hear our prayers. He who made the family as his chosen instrument to communicate physical life desires to use the same family as his special instrument to communicate spiritual life: grace builds upon and perfects nature.

The Spiritual Sense

Not surprisingly, this passage about Jairus and the woman also has a profound allegorical sense, as St. Bede and St. Ambrose both notice in their commentaries on St. Luke's Gospel. According to this allegory, Jairus, since he is the leader of the synagogue, represents the Jewish leaders. His daughter represents the Jewish people, and the woman with a hemorrhage represents the gentile people. Jairus's daughter has lived for twelve years in the home of her father, and this signifies that the Jewish people had lived within the Jewish church during the whole time of the covenant with the twelve tribes of Israel (the Mosaic covenant; see Exodus 34:27). On the other hand, the gentiles were excluded from this covenant (unlike the covenants made with Adam and Noah that included all their descendants, Jew and Gentile alike). Thus, the woman is said to have a flow of blood for the same amount of time, twelve years, to signify that during the time of the Mosaic covenant the gentiles were unclean and excluded from the assembly of God.

During that time they spent all their substance on physicians; that is, they sought in vain for salvation from philosophy or false gods. But now that the time of Christ has come, the reality was to replace the figure. Therefore, those who sought salvation in the letter of the law rather than in faith in Jesus, to whom the law pointed, were spiritually dying: for "the letter kills while the spirit gives life" (2 Cor. 3:6). Yet the gentiles touched the hem of Jesus' garment from behind, since they did not come into contact with Jesus in person, or face-to-face. As he himself testified: "I was sent only to the lost sheep of the house of Israel" (Matt. 15:24). Rather, after the Ascension of Jesus, they followed after him and came into contact with him through the teaching of his disciples and through the sacraments, which are signified by his garment. On the other hand, because the Jewish leaders did not put perfect faith in Jesus at the beginning, the Jewish people under their care suffered spiritual death.

Nevertheless, they are not abandoned by Christ; as St. Paul expressly teaches, "the gifts and the call of God are irrevocable" (Rom. 11:29). But before the Jewish people are to be raised up to life again, it was necessary that salvation come first to the gentiles through faith in Jesus: "a hardening has come upon part of Israel, until the full number of the gentiles come in, and so all Israel will be saved" (Rom. 11:25–26). This is signified by Jesus healing the woman and calling her his daughter on the way to raise up the daughter of Jairus. Finally, Jesus comes and raises up the Jewish people, and instructs that she should be given something to eat, namely the Eucharist, when they partake fully of the unity of the Catholic Church, in that are united once again, Jew and Gentile alike.

Being Evangelized by the
Conversation with Jairus

How do you come to Jesus? Do you make him your last resort? And when you do come to him, do you need to feel his presence throughout your trials and difficulties in life? The faith of the centurion is something truly admirable, and it is that kind of faith that Jesus wants to draw out from us.

And what about our compassion for others: Do we see the needs of all of God's children, or are we so fixated on our own problems (or lack thereof) that we do not notice the suffering of others.

Evangelizing by Means of the Conversation with Jairus

Most of the people we will encounter who desire to come to know Jesus begin with very imperfect motives and very imperfect trust. They will come to Jesus because they need something from him: help for a loved one, health, financial security. Moreover, they will often suffer from great fear: fear that Jesus cannot help them; fear that Jesus does not want to help them; fear that Jesus will not help them the way they want to be helped. Our role as evangelists in such cases involves imparting a sense of security and trust to those who are afraid. We must assure them that the Lord will make everything turn out well, better than we could ever hope, but in his time. And if we can just believe this from the beginning, we will live in joy and hope, not demanding that we see the results we want right away, and not requiring that we feel the presence of Jesus along the way.

Most of our sufferings are self-inflicted, yet with all our limitations, even if we cannot trust him perfectly, and even if we add to our own sufferings, the Lord is faithful! We must repeat this over and over again: the Lord is faithful!

CHAPTER 10

THE LAZY SERVANT

In Matthew's Gospel, Jesus tells a series of judgment parables. One of these is about the servants in God's household. The parable reads as follows:

[The Kingdom of Heaven] will be as when a man who was going on a journey called in his servants and entrusted his possessions to them. To one he gave five talents; to another, two; to a third, one—to each according to his ability. Then he went away. Immediately the one who received five talents went and traded with them, and made another five. Likewise, the one who received two made another two. But the man who received one went off and dug a hole in the ground and buried his master's money.

After a long time, the master of those servants came back and settled accounts with them. The one who had received five talents came forward bringing the additional five. He said, "Master, you gave me five talents. See, I have made five more." His master said to him, "Well done, my good and faithful servant. Since you were faithful in small matters, I will give you great responsibilities. Come, share your master's joy." [Then] the one who had received two talents also came forward and said, "Master, you gave me two talents. See, I have made two more." His master said to him, "Well done, my good and faithful servant. Since you were faithful in small matters, I will give you great responsibilities. Come, share your master's joy."

Then the one who had received the one talent came forward and said, "Master, I knew you were a demanding person, harvesting where you did not plant and gathering where you did not scatter; so out of fear I went off and buried your talent in the ground. Here it is back." His master said to him in reply, "You wicked, lazy servant! So you knew that I harvest where I did not plant and gather where I did not scatter? Should you not then have put my money in the bank so that I could have got it back with interest on my return? Now then! Take the talent from him and give it to the one with ten. For to everyone who has, more will be given and he will grow rich; but from the one who has not, even what he has will be taken away. And throw this useless servant into the darkness outside, where there will be wailing and grinding of teeth" (Matt. 25:14–30).

The Context of the Parable

Jesus is on the brink of his Passion and death. He is about to depart from this world, so he prepares his disciples by instructing them about the Last Things: death, judgment, heaven, hell. So Jesus tells a series of parables about the judgment. More specifically, in order to prepare his disciples for his imminent Passion, Jesus tells them a parable about the departure and return of the master. The parable focuses upon the different attitudes a disciple can have toward God. Some see God as a generous benefactor, others as a harsh master. The parable also addresses the final judgment at the

Second Coming, and it focuses upon the judgment of the servants; that is, members of God's household who knew the master. This parable, then, does not seem to be so much about the judgment of unbelievers, but of believers.

The Literal Sense

The master in the parable is God, the servants are those who are members of his household; that is, members of his Church. The possessions refer to the created goods and gifts that God has distributed to each member of the Church.[30] The first thing to notice is that the master *entrusted his possessions* to his servants. This is an act of confidence and generosity that is meant to inspire hope and gratitude in the hearts of his servants. For when someone entrusts his possessions to another, he is treating that other as another self, as a friend.

He does not entrust each servant with an equal amount of his possessions, but with an unequal amount: *according to their ability.* God distributes his gifts unequally because he wants his goodness to be reflected more perfectly in creation. For if God gave the same gifts to each, then the same aspect of God's goodness would be reflected in each one, so that his goodness would not be reflected more in a multitude than in a single individual. But by distributing different gifts to different individuals, a different aspect of God's goodness is reflected in each so that there is no redundancy. Thus, a greater share in God's goodness is reflected in the diverse multitude than in each individual. Correspondingly to his diverse gifts, God also gives diverse abilities, since whenever he calls someone to accomplish some good, he also grants them the ability to fulfill what he asks. Notice too that even those who receive lesser abilities and gifts still reflect something of God's goodness that those with greater gifts do not, for their gifts are not merely less, but also different. In God's original plan, no one is useless or expendable. Each is like a different flower in the garden of God's creation.[31]

The parable then recounts how each servant used his talents. First, it mentions that they went *immediately*. Promptness in fulfilling the will of God is a sign of devotion and good will. And this is the first thing we must do when we become aware of God's will for us. The first two servants, although their gifts were unequal, nevertheless strove with equal industriousness. And so each one doubled his master's possessions. Five talents became ten, and two talents became four. But it seems that this involved some injustice. For if by trading one receives back more than he gave, this seems to be an unjust exchange. But it should be understood that the goods in question are not material goods, but rather spiritual goods. For these are the true possessions that Christ has entrusted to us. And unlike material goods, spiritual goods are increased when they are exchanged and given away. For when a man teaches another, he does not lose his knowledge, but rather is confirmed in it and even grows in knowledge the more he teaches. And when a man shares his faith, he does not diminish, but rather grows in faith. And when a man gives his love to another, he does not lose his love, but increases it.

But the last servant who had received one talent did not trade with it, but rather dug a hole in the ground and buried his master's money. This was not because he received less than the others, for the servant who received two talents, though he too received less, traded and doubled his goods just as the servant with five had done. But since the talent signifies spiritual goods rather than material goods, what does it mean to dig a hole in the ground and bury the money? The ground signifies the earthly part of human nature, which seeks only its own good rather than the good of our neighbor.

Therefore, to dig a hole in the ground and bury the master's money signifies choosing to follow earthly desires so that the spiritual gifts given to him are never used to benefit anyone else. They are such slaves to sensual desire that they use their spiritual gifts to satisfy their flesh. Jesus describes such souls when he says, "The one who is of the earth is earthly and speaks of earthly things" (John 3:31). St. Paul too speaks of men like this, describing them as "men with corrupted minds . . . supposing religion to be a means of gain" (1 Tim. 6:5).

Next, the parable tells of the return of the master *after a long time*. The time that the master is away is said to be long because God gives much time and many opportunities to his servants both to do good and repent from evil. This is why St. Peter says, "He is patient with you, not wishing that any should perish but that all should come to repentance" (2 Pet. 3:9). But after that time comes the reckoning; that is, the judgment of each soul before God for the good or evil he has done in this life.

The first servant comes willingly before his master and reports: *Master, you gave me five talents. See, I have made five more.* He begins by addressing the master, and in doing this he is acknowledging his primacy and generosity. *For this servant, the judgment is all about the goodness of his master.* He is eager to give back to the master the goods he has earned as a sign of his gratitude. He does not deny that he was responsible for the increase. He says *I have made five more.* But he recognizes that his contribution depended first upon the master's generosity.

Sometimes I encounter people who are striving for greater humility. And they mistakenly think that humility means denying any responsibility for the good they have done. For example, in response to a compliment, they say something like, "Oh no, I didn't do anything good." But the problem with that attitude is that it fails to acknowledge that God has accomplished a good in us. Under the pretense of false humility, such a person ends up refusing to acknowledge God's goodness. So the proper response to a compliment is "Thank you. Thanks be to God that he has used me to bring about this good."

In response to his servant's gratitude and confidence, the master says to him: *Well done, my good and faithful servant. Since you were faithful in small matters, I will give you great responsibilities. Come, share your master's joy.* First the master praises and acknowledges the goodness and fidelity of his servant. This shall be the greatest blessing the elect shall receive at the final judgment: to be praised by God, to know that we are good and faithful because God has made us to be so. Then the master speaks of the reward for fidelity, and this reward far outstrips the labor the servant has employed: our fidelity will be in *small matters* but our reward will be *great.* This signifies that the rewards of heaven are exceedingly great compared to the labors of this life. As St. Paul says, "I consider that the sufferings of this present time are as nothing compared with the glory to be revealed for us" (Rom. 8:18). Yet even though the rewards of heaven are exceedingly great compared to our labors because of God's mercy, nevertheless there remains a kind of proportion in which God's justice is reflected.

Thus, Peter says, "Rejoice in the measure that you share Christ's sufferings, when his glory is revealed, you will rejoice exultantly" (1 Pet. 4:13). Finally, the master invites him to enter into his joy. He does not say that joy enters into him, but that he enters into joy, as if it is a joy that is greater than the soul can contain. This is eternal salvation, and hope for this joy is what gives the good servant energy and perseverance to accomplish the master's will. The judgment for the next servant is the same, even though he had received fewer talents.

But then comes the reckoning of the servant who buried his master's money: *Then the one who had received the one talent came forward and said, "Master, I knew you . . ."* Like the first two servants, he acknowledges his master; but then instead of acknowledging with gratitude the gifts he had received from his master, he claims to know the full truth about his master. He says *I knew you* as if his knowledge were the ultimate foundation of truth. And so this servant puts himself at the center of the judgment, makes himself the judge, and pronounces sentence. For this servant, the judgment is not about the goodness of the master, but about his perceived defects.

He accuses his master of three defects. The first is that he was demanding. The Greek text says "hard." In other words, according to the judgment of this servant, his master was inflexible and lacking in compassion. He did not care about his servant. The second defect was that he harvested where he did not plant. When someone plants a seed, he places it carefully in ground where it will grow. Thus, one who harvests where he did not plant is one who demands good results from someone when he did not provide the circumstances for success. The third defect is that he gathered where he did not scatter. To scatter is to freely throw seeds, which are the principles of all living things.

Thus, one who gathers where he did not scatter is one who demands good results without even providing the most basic and necessary starting material, without even providing the seeds. In summary, this servant accuses his master of providing nothing, and demanding everything, so that it was impossible for the servant to do any good under the conditions provided by the master.

After judging his master, the servant then excuses himself: *so out of fear I went off and buried your talent in the ground. Here it is back.* He claims to have done no injustice because he was afraid, and he returns what he was given. But the truth is that the master had provided everything necessary for the servant to succeed, and the servant had a duty to work on behalf of his master. For a servant who gives back what he had received is no better than a hole in the ground. So in reality the servant had done an injustice to his master because he was both ungrateful and lazy. The parable goes on to note what his master said to him in reply: *You wicked, lazy servant!*

And even though the servant had falsely accused the master of being hard and demanding, the master does not defend himself, but merely judges the servant based upon his own assertions: *So you knew that I harvest where I did not plant and gather where I did not scatter? Should you not then have put my money in the bank so that I could have got it back with interest on my return?* God will act toward us as we judge him to be. If we judge him to be merciful, he will act mercifully toward us. If we judge him to be harsh, he will act harshly toward us. For this reason it is said about God in the Psalms: "With the sincere you show yourself sincere, but the cunning you outdo in cunning" (Ps. 18:27).

But what does it mean when the master says that he should have at least put his money in the bank so he could have it back with interest? What do the bank and the interest signify? A banker is one who does the investing on our behalf, and interest is the share of the profit made by the banker. Therefore, putting the master's money in the bank signifies subjecting ourselves to others who can direct the use of the spiritual goods given to us by God. Or perhaps another interpretation could be consecrating ourselves to the Virgin Mary so that she might apply the merits of our works where she sees fit, since she is a supremely wise banker in spiritual matters.

Last of all, the parable tells of the punishment inflicted upon the lazy servant: *Now then! Take the talent from him and give it to the one with ten. For to everyone who has, more will be given and he will grow rich; but from the one who has not, even what he has will be taken away. And throw this useless servant into the darkness outside, where there will be wailing and grinding of teeth.* The first part of the punishment is that what he has been given is taken away. For it is just that when someone has misused his ability this ability be taken away from him. The second part of the punishment is that the useless servant is thrown outside into the darkness; that is, he will be deprived of the light of divine truth. And this is fitting since he falsely judged his master by his own apprehension of truth, which was actually error and darkness. And instead of the joy of the good servants, who forever sing the praises of God, there will be sadness for this bad servant who will use his mouth not to praise God, but to bewail his own wickedness.

Notice too that the talent taken from the lazy servant is given to the one with ten talents. This signifies first of all that nothing of God's gifts are lost. If some abuse them, God bestows them freely upon others so that nothing of God's goodness shall be lost in creation. St. Faustina once recorded these words of Jesus in her diary: "I want to give myself to souls and to fill them with my love, but few there are who want to accept all the graces my love has intended for them. My grace is not lost; if the soul for whom it was intended does not accept it, another soul takes it."[32] Second, this shows that the Lord sometimes rewards not only in proportion to our merits, but even above that due by our merits.

The master then gives a reason for his decision: *For to everyone who has, more will be given and he will grow rich; but from the one who has not, even what he has will be taken away.* The lazy servant treated his talents as something to be preserved for his own protection, and this is to see the gifts of God as if they were desirable to make profit for ourselves, rather than desirable for the sake of doing the master's will. And one who treats the gifts of God as if they possessed complete goodness in themselves rather than seeing them as a sign of the goodness they borrow from God does not truly possess them, just as a miser who loves money for its own sake and refuses to spend it does not truly possess that money.

This is why the Lord says that this servant both "has" and "has not." He "has" insofar as he is able to experience the created goodness of these creatures for a time, but he "has not" inasmuch as the true and lasting worth of those created goods escapes him. And eventually, this defective kind of possession will be taken away, since the created goods in which he hoped for happiness will eventually be taken from him as well. For just as it is true that those who seek first the kingdom of God will receive all other created goods besides, so also those who seek first the things of this world will not inherit the kingdom of God, nor any created goods besides.

The words of the Lord in this parable are very much like the words Jesus said earlier to the apostles concerning why he had taught them openly, whereas to the multitude he spoke in parables: "Whosoever has, it will be given to him, and he will be made to abound; but whoever does not have, even what he has will be taken away from him" (Matt. 13:12). This indicates that this parable should be interpreted in light of what the Lord says in that place. In this case, the talents would especially signify the divine truths of our faith, which are given openly to some because they have been found worthy, but are hidden from others because they are not worthy.

Looking back upon this parable, we do well to ask what is the sin of the lazy servant? He is faced with a choice: either he can put effort into trying to do a good, with the risk that he might fail (trading his talent); or he can simply avoid an evil without effort or risk of failure (burying his talent). In the end, he is more afraid of doing evil than of omitting good. This is instructive since it reveals that *the spiritual life is primarily about doing good, not primarily about avoiding evil!*[33] So one lesson we can learn from this parable is that it is extremely important to take risks for the sake of doing good.

But that brings us to another question: What about the risk? Why isn't there a story about a servant who trades and loses his master's money? Here again, what the parable doesn't say is as instructive as what it does say. I think that the fact that there is no servant who trades and fails is an indication of the generosity of God, who does not permit those who try to serve him to fail in doing spiritual good. It may be that they seem to lack success from the point of an external observer; but God calls us to be faithful, not successful in the eyes of the world. So long as one seeks to do God's will with love, one cannot fail to grow in love. Unlike physical goods, spiritual goods multiply by the fact of their being exercised. And therefore, what seems like a risk from the viewpoint of the servant is destined to always succeed from the viewpoint of the master who always gives more than enough to his servants: "For God is at work in you, both to will and to work for his good pleasure" (Phil. 2:13).

One cannot help but think that Jesus was thinking of Judas Iscariot when he told this parable. It was shortly before his Passion and Judas had already made up his mind to betray him. Jesus had showered his grace upon Judas, giving him the grace to be an apostle. Jesus promised Judas the gift of himself in the Eucharist, but Judas buried this great treasure in earthly thoughts.[34] Besides, Judas was the one who held the common purse for the community and had been unfaithful in this duty (John 12:6), so this parable seems to have special applicability to Judas, seeming like a subtle warning to him in hopes of converting him. Each of us has a Judas dwelling in his heart. Each of us should be willing to heed this admonition of the Lord to confess our sins, and begin again to believe in the goodness of our master.

Being Evangelized by the
Parable of the Lazy Servant

How do we perceive the Lord? Do we think of him as an exacting and harsh master who has set us up for inevitable failure? Or do we see him as he is: a generous master who has equipped us superabundantly for every mission? This makes all the difference. And if we do not see him as generous, as waiting to bring us joy, we need to undergo a deep conversion of heart.

Do we take risks in our service to the Lord in order to achieve the greatest goods? Or are we afraid to fail? Does our fear make us lazy in our service to the Lord? Here again, if we are not taking risks to grow in faith and love, to share our faith and love, we need to undergo a deep conversion. We need to acquire the virtue of magnanimity: greatness of soul.

Evangelizing by Means of the
Parable of the Lazy Servant

This parable is directed toward those who are already employed in the service of the Lord, so it is not about evangelizing the unevangelized, but rather about evangelizing the imperfectly evangelized. The first thing that a servant of the Lord must recognize and gratefully accept is that God distributes his gifts unequally; that is, he gives different gifts to different people. This should not be the occasion of envy or discouragement. We must love above all things the common good of the Church, rather than putting our private good first. God gave the same praise to the servant who doubled his two talents as to the one who had doubled five. The important thing is that we do what we can with the gifts we have been given.

Second, in evangelizing fellow servants of Christ, we should help them to focus primarily upon the spiritual goods they accomplish rather than in the appearance of material success. We can falsely think that if we raise a lot of money for the parish, or get a lot of positive publicity, or have a lot of social media followers, then we are succeeding. That's not true: God calls us to be faithful, not successful in the eyes of the world.

Finally, we should help others to see that being a good servant of the Lord means seeing God as a generous Lord, and that our primary focus must be upon doing good with manifest joy. The Lord God "loves a cheerful giver" (2 Cor. 9:7).

CHAPTER 11

THE LABORERS
WHO COME LATE

The perception that God is unfair to those who serve him is something that Christians have always struggled with. In order to explain God's justice in his dealings with his servants, Jesus tells his disciples the following parable:

The Kingdom of Heaven is like a landowner who went out at dawn to hire laborers for his vineyard. After agreeing with them for the usual daily wage, he sent them into his vineyard. Going out about nine o'clock, he saw others standing idle in the marketplace, and he said to them, "You too go into my vineyard, and I will give you what is just." So they went off. [And] he went out again around noon, and around three o'clock, and did likewise. Going out about five o'clock, he found others standing around, and said to them, "Why do you stand here idle all day?" They answered, "Because no one has hired us." He said to them, "You too go into my vineyard."

When it was evening the owner of the vineyard said to his foreman, "Summon the laborers and give them their pay, beginning with the last and ending with the first." When those who had started about five o'clock came, each received the usual daily wage. So when the first came, they thought that they would receive more, but each of them also got the usual wage. And on receiving it they grumbled against the landowner, saying, "These last ones worked only one hour, and you have made them equal to us, who bore the day's burden and the heat."

He said to one of them in reply, "My friend, I am not cheating you. Did you not agree with me for the usual daily wage? Take what is yours and go. What if I wish to give this last one the same as you? [Or] am I not free to do as I wish with my own money? Are you envious because I am generous?" Thus, the last will be first, and the first will be last (Matt. 20:1–16).

The Context of the Parable

This parable comes at the beginning of the twentieth chapter of the Gospel according to St. Matthew. In the nineteenth chapter, Jesus admonishes the disciples to let the little children come to him, since to them belongs the kingdom of heaven. Then the rich young man comes to ask Jesus about salvation, but he refuses Jesus' invitation to sell all and follow him. The last line of chapter nineteen reads: "many that are first shall be last, and the last shall be first" (19:30). So before telling this parable, Jesus is pointing out that those who are small in the eyes of the world, without wealth or power or influence, are going to be first, whereas many of those who do have these things will be last in the kingdom of heaven. Moreover, after Jesus tells this parable, the disciples break out into an argument about who will be first in the kingdom. Once again, Jesus has to instruct them that to be first means to be last: to serve the rest, to look to the good of others before your own.

There are many ways to be first and last: first in power, wealth, authority. The parable about the laborers refers to those who are first and last in time of service: namely, those who have served from the beginning, perhaps throughout their entire lives, and those who, due to a late conversion, have only served at the end of their lives. So this parable is more specifically told for the benefit of those who have faithfully served the Lord for the greater part of their lives at great personal sacrifice. Like the previous parable, this parable is addressed to believers, servants of Jesus Christ. And it is a fact of experience that when we see those who have lived a life dedicated to following their own desires suddenly converted, perhaps even on their deathbed, the perception of injustice creeps into our souls. Both envy and the desire to judge another is a constant temptation in the face of such seeming injustice. But let us return to the parable and see whether this envy and spirit of judgment is warranted.

The Literal Sense

The parable stresses the initiative of the master. He it is who goes out at dawn, at midmorning, at noon, at midafternoon, and finally in the evening. Unless he had gone out to find laborers, they would not have had the opportunity to receive the *usual daily wage*. The parable reveals God's initiative in freely giving his grace to different persons at different points in their lives. The previous parable spoke of the inequality of God's gifts; here too there is an inequality in the time in that each is called, though there is no inequality in the reward. This inequality is willed by God in his provident wisdom for the sake of the common good. When he gets to the last ones, the master asks them a question: *Going out about five o'clock, he found others standing around, and said to them, "Why do you stand here idle all day?" They answered, "Because no one has hired us." He said to them, "You too go into my vineyard."* It is true that they have stood there idle the whole day, over the entire course of their life, yet it is because no one has hired them. That is, they have not received the invitation of God's grace. The master does not reject them or chastise them for their laziness, but rather freely invites them to labor in his vineyard, even for a short while.

Finally, the day is over and the reckoning comes (which signifies the final judgment after the labors of this life are over) and a reward is bestowed upon those who have labored in the vineyard of this world. Beginning with those who came last, the wage is given; but it is the same wage given to all. And this appears to involve an injustice. For injustice happens when those who are unequal are treated as if they were equal, or when those who are equal are treated as if they were unequal. And this is just what the laborers say who had worked the entire day: *These last ones worked only one hour, and you have made them equal to us, who bore the day's burden and the heat.* That is, you have treated those who are unequal as if they were equal.

But the master points out in response that he has done no injustice by being more merciful to some than to others. For he did not deny them a just wage; rather, in his generosity, he gave more than what is just to those who worked less. But this is not injustice: rather it proceeds from mercy that "triumphs over justice" (James 2:13). And the master points out the true cause of their perceived injustice: envy. *Are you envious because I am generous?*

We do well to consider the root causes of envy, so that we can uproot it from our hearts. Envy can be defined as deliberate or chosen sorrow at the good of another. As a sin, envy is very mysterious, since it makes you sad. At least with other sins, like gluttony, you get something out of it, some pleasure. But envy makes you sad. It is like paying someone good money to hurt you. So it's very hard to see the attractiveness of envy. Envy is a lose-lose situation.

Among sins, envy has a certain preeminence. The scriptures teach that "through the envy of the devil death entered into the world" (Wis. 2:24). Envy holds this preeminence because it is contrary to the good and to rightly ordered love in every possible way. First, envy is contrary to our own good and love of self, since it makes us sad. Second, envy is contrary to the good and love of our neighbor because we desire that they be deprived of their good through envy. But if we truly loved our neighbor as ourselves, we would be just as happy to see them possess some good as if we possessed it. But most important, envy is contrary to love of God, and it prevents us from appreciating God's goodness: *Are you envious because I am generous?* The envious man does not delight in God's generosity, for he will love and appreciate only the goods that God has given to him, not the goods God has given to others. But the goods that belong to a single creature are infinitesimal compared to the goods that God has conferred upon the whole of creation. And trying to appreciate God's goodness based solely on the goods he has given to us is like trying to do geometry when the only thing you admit exists is a point.

So why do we fall into the sin of envy? Usually it is because of some perceived injustice. The laborers who worked all day are made equal to the laborers who worked an hour. How is that just? The older brother of the prodigal son had the same complaint: he spent all his money on prostitutes and loose living, and for him you slaughter the fatted calf?! But if we examine the question carefully, we will see how deceived we are when we envy God's gifts in others.

Let's take an extreme example: someone who has lived a completely vicious life, has indulged in every pleasure, pursued all his desires, has even hurt you and your loved ones, is suddenly converted at the end of his life, and obtains so great a degree of charity that he ends up with a higher place in heaven than you. That seems completely unfair. But the truth is that it is fair.

The root, the ultimate reason for merit is charity, not difficulty or suffering. We tend to think that the harder some task is, the more merit it deserves. And certainly persevering through some difficult, good work is a sign of great love. But it is the love itself rather than the sign of the love that deserves reward. Simon of Cyrene carried Jesus' cross, but St. Veronica just wiped his face. Yet the compassion of St. Veronica seems to have merited more than the labors of Simon, since the Church immediately recognized her as a saint, whereas the question was in doubt about Simon because he was pressed into service. So it is not necessarily true that one who has suffered more and labored more for the kingdom will have a greater reward in heaven; rather, the one who loves more will enjoy the greater reward.

But what if this person hurt you and those whom you love: Doesn't that deserve punishment? As a consequence of his greater charity, his contrition is so great that he is more pained at having hurt you than you are in being hurt. It is not as if he gets away without being punished. And due to his greater love he's more sorry for his sins than you are for yours. "I tell you, her sins, which are many, are forgiven, for she loved much; but he who is forgiven little, loves little" (Luke 7:47). So the reward God gives is still fair.

Finally, no injustice is done to one who has labored more for the kingdom. What were the laborers who came late doing before they began to serve the Lord? They were trapped in their sins, standing idle all day. Once they are converted, they shall not look back with fondness on that time of their life, but with a certain sadness. How is it then that a true servant of the Lord shall look with envy on the life of those others spent in idleness and sin, compared to their own life of fruitful labor for the kingdom?

More important, what is the "usual daily wage" signified by this parable? It is nothing other than the vision of God, the happiness of God! And this reward far exceeds all the merit of our labors. The truth is that we should be glad to show our gratitude for so great a gift as salvation. If a poor peasant were chosen by a beautiful and virtuous princess for her spouse, he would long to have some way of showing her that he is worthy of her. Any real man in those circumstances would want to perform some great deed to manifest his worth. The truth is that we should even feel a little sorry for those who did not have the opportunity to labor and bear the heat of the day. There will be a certain joy that those who labored most shall experience in being able to do as much as they could to manifest their appreciation for the gift of eternal life.

In the final analysis, what is the cause of envy? And how can we avoid envy? The root cause of envy is the preference for private goods over common goods. A private good is one that is diminished when shared, or sometimes can't be shared at all. You can't wear my socks while I am wearing my socks. I can't eat this piece of pizza if you eat it. Material goods cause strife and envy, then, because they can't be shared without being diminished.

In contrast, a common good can be shared by many without being diminished. If I teach you some truth, then not only do you have it when I give it to you, but I do not lose it. In fact, I have it more firmly because I have taught it to you. Common goods are even increased when they are shared, not diminished. Such common goods are spiritual, not material, and they include truth, love, virtue, and God.

In the parable of the prodigal son, the inheritance had to be divided when it was shared: it was a private good. Hence, it was a cause of strife between the brothers and it separated the sons from their father. But the true good that both brothers ought to have been seeking first was the father's love. The father's love was not diminished, but rather increased, by loving both brothers. The desire to possess common goods does not cause envy or strife because there is no opposition between your possessing them and my possessing them. If we both love common goods the most, then envy will find no place in our hearts.

The Allegorical Sense

This same passage can be read in an allegorical sense to refer to the plan of salvation set forth for both the Jews and the gentile nations. Here the *landowner* is God. He is said to go *out at dawn* to *hire laborers for his vineyard*, because at the dawn of creation God entrusted man with the task of caring for the earth and subduing it to God through reasonable activity. Thus, we read in the book of Genesis: "Be fertile and multiply; fill the earth and subdue it. Have dominion over the fish of the sea, the birds of the air, and all the living things that move on the earth. . . . See, I give you every seed-bearing plant all over the earth and every tree that has seed-bearing fruit on it to be your food; and to all the animals of the land, all the birds of the air, and all the living creatures that crawl on the ground, I give all the green plants for food" (Gen. 1:27–30).

The *usual daily wage* is the reward promised by God to all those who keep his commandments: eternal life. This was the beginning of the promises made to the chosen people, which culminated in the covenants made to Abraham and Moses. Or perhaps *dawn* may be taken to signify the day of the Resurrection, when the Lord first sent out his apostles into the world to go first to the house of Israel. For St. Luke had recounted that when Jesus appeared to his disciples after his Resurrection that "repentance and forgiveness of sins should be preached in his name to all nations, beginning from Jerusalem" (Luke 24:47).

But then the landowner goes out again. This signifies the constant initiative of God in salvation. He renews over and over again his covenant, and enters into the world by means of his grace. God also goes out through his minsters: missionaries who bring his word to those who have not yet been evangelized. He is said to go out at different times: nine o'clock, noon, three o'clock, and five o'clock. This signifies the various times in the history of the world when the gentile nations were evangelized. Each time, he sends laborers into his vineyard. These laborers had stood idle, and they signify the gentile nations, who had not yet been visited by God or employed in his service. This time, he does not agree with them for the usual daily wage, but rather he says that he will give them *what is just.* This signifies that the gentile nations did not receive the same promises as did the Jewish people.

When it was evening the owner of the vineyard said to his foreman, "Summon the laborers and give them their pay." This signifies the final judgment, when the foreman—that is, the angel of the final resurrection—shall summon all the faithful together at the sound of a trumpet: "The Lord himself, with a word of command, with the voice of an archangel and with the trumpet of God, will come down from heaven, and the dead in Christ will rise first" (1 Thess. 4:16). And although they did not receive the same promise as the Jews, they did receive the same reward, not from a promise, but from God's mercy and largesse.

Finally, the envy of the Jewish people is related: *Are you envious because I am generous?* Yet this envy becomes the means of their conversion to Christ by which they were finally to be saved at the end of the world, as St. Paul teaches in Romans: "Did not Israel understand? First Moses says, 'I will make you jealous of those who are not a nation; with a senseless nation I will make you angry'" (Rom. 10:19). And a little further on he concludes: "A hardening has come upon Israel in part, until the full number of the gentiles comes in, and thus all Israel will be saved" (Rom. 11:25–26). Thus, *the last will be first*—that is, those to whom the gospel was preached last will be saved first—and *the first will be last*; that is, those to whom the gospel was preached first will be saved last.

Being Evangelized by the Parable About the Laborers Who Come Late

Being evangelized by this parable requires that we see the primacy of mercy and divine grace in the spiritual life. It means recognizing that, if justice were the only factor in our relationship with the Lord, then all of us deserve eternal separation from God, born as we were in original sin. And therefore, the fact that we got hired at all, and promised the usual daily wage of eternal life, is simply an unmerited gift of unimaginable worth. From the point that we have been employed in the service of the Lord, our disposition must be: may the Lord have mercy on all, and may others receive even greater mercy than me!

Evangelizing by Means of the Parable About the Laborers Who Come Late

This parable too is directed toward the servants of the Lord, not unbelievers. So it is helpful primarily for the "partially evangelized." On the one hand, we should show understanding and compassion to those who feel that they have labored so much more than others and yet received a recompense not proportional to their labors. This was how Martha felt when she complained to the Lord about Mary: "Lord, do you not care that my sister has left me by myself to do the serving?" (Luke 10:40). We must reassure them that the Lord does care about them and is pleased by their labors. At the same time, we must ask them this question: "Are you working for the glory of the Lord or your own glory?" We as servants must have our eyes on the Lord, not on one another. We should focus upon our relationship with him rather than on our comparison with them. We should remind them too that the reward promised by the Lord is also disproportionate to their labors, and that it is a great blessing to be able to manifest our gratitude by doing what we can with all our strength.

CHAPTER 12

THE PRODIGAL SON

The themes of ingratitude and envy that figure prominently in the previous two parables are found also in the famous parable of the prodigal son. And here these perennial problems of the spiritual life seem to find an even more profound resolution. Of all the parables of the Lord, this is perhaps the most beautiful and the most moving. Who knows what a great multitude of the elect were converted and saved through this one parable?

A certain man had two sons. And the younger of them said to his father: "Father, give me the portion of the substance that falls to me." And he divided his substance to them. And not many days later, the younger son, gathering everything together, went abroad into a far country; and there wasted his substance, living irresponsibly. And after he had spent everything, there came a great famine in that country; and he began to be in want. And he went and cleaved to one of the citizens of that country. And he sent him into his farm to feed swine. And he longed to fill his belly with the husks the swine were eating, but no one gave him anything. And returning to himself, he said, "How many hired servants in my father's house abound with bread, and here I perish with hunger. I will arise and go to my father, and say to him: 'Father, I have sinned against heaven and before you. I am not worthy to be called your son. Make me as one of your hired servants.'" And rising up he came to his father.

And when he was still a long way off, his father saw him, and was moved with compassion. And running to him, he fell upon his neck and kissed him. And the son said to him: "Father, I have sinned against heaven and before you. I am not now worthy to be called your son." And the father said to his servants: "Quickly, bring forth the first robe, and put it on him; and put a ring on his hand, and shoes on his feet. And bring here the fatted calf, and kill it, and let us eat and make merry. Because this, my son, was dead and is come to life again; he was lost and is found." And they began to make merry.

Now the elder son was in the field. And when he drew near to the house, he heard music and dancing. And he called one of the servants and asked what these things meant. And he said to him: Your brother has come, and your father has killed the fatted calf, because he has received him safe. And he was filled with wrath and would not go in. Therefore, his father coming out began to entreat him. And he, answering, said to his father: "Look, for so many years I am serving you, and I have never transgressed your commandment. And yet you have never given me a young goat to make merry with my friends. But as soon as this, your son, is come, who has devoured his substance with harlots, you killed for him the fatted calf."

But he said to him: "Son, you are always with me, and all I have is yours. But it was fitting that that we should make merry and be glad, for this, your brother, was dead and is come to life again; he was lost and is found" (Luke 15:11–32).

The Context of the Parable

At the beginning of the fifteenth chapter of the Gospel according to St. Luke, it says, "Now publicans and sinners drew near to [Jesus] to hear him. And the Pharisees and scribes murmured saying: 'This man receives sinners and eats with them.'" In response to this accusation, Jesus tells three parables about God's mercy, the last of which is the parable of the prodigal son. The other two parables preceding this one are about a lost sheep and a lost coin. Right away, that implies that the third parable should be read as a parable about a lost son. Each parable makes an argument that what is lost should be sought and found, and rejoiced over when it is found.

At the heart of each argument is a basic fact: the goodness of what is lost. The lost sheep is good, the lost coin is good, the lost son is good. God our Father sees us through the eyes of his own goodness: he sees his own goodness in us. And so he sees our worth as something truly good, truly worth the trouble of saving. The Pharisees and scribes, on the other hand, cannot perceive the goodness of those who are lost; and ironically, therefore lose sight of their own goodness and even of God's goodness.

Perhaps the Pharisees and the scribes think that the lost sheep and lost coin are only about the publicans and sinners with whom Jesus is eating; but the parable of the lost son reveals that the elder son may be more lost than the younger one. Perhaps the ones who are more truly lost and in need of being found are the Pharisees and scribes. If we have a hard time seeing why sinners should be sought after, perhaps this parable is necessary to correct our vision of the world. Perhaps we need it to see once again the goodness of the sinner, the goodness of ourselves, and the goodness of our Father in heaven.

The Literal Sense

The first thing to realize about the younger son is that he wasn't just a young man who wanted to set out on his own, sow his oats, or stretch his wings. No, he *hated his father.* How do we know this? Because he asks for his inheritance early, even though as the younger son he has less of a right to it. When do you normally receive your inheritance? When your father dies. In this case, then, the son was saying to his father: "As far as I'm concerned, I wish you were dead." Moreover, after he receives his inheritance, as soon as he can, he goes as far away as he can: *Not many days later . . . he went abroad into a far country.* He was not planning on coming home for Christmas or Thanksgiving. He never wanted to see his father ever again.

So that was the disposition of the son to his father who gave him life. Now, the father could have said, "No, you're asking for something unreasonable." Or he could have simply told him: "You are a spoiled brat: see how far you get without any money." But he did not want his son to be without some means of support, seeing that he had made up his mind to go. And so in his goodness and generosity, the father gives him everything he asks for, even though that meant losing much of his wealth. The father acts as if he had in fact died and handed over the inheritance to his son.

This is how our Father in heaven treats us when we reject him, even when we hate him. He still provides us with the created goods that we need lest we utterly despair and perish. Though we reject him out of our love for the things he gives us, he does not refuse to give them to us anyway, in the hope that one day the remembrance of his generosity will restore our confidence in his goodness and love for us.

Sometimes concerned parents ask me whether they should provide means of support for their wayward children. Their son is living with a woman in college, and they feel that paying his rent is enabling him. Or their daughter is taking drugs, and they feel that providing her with money for food is making this possible. In such cases I tell them: do not give them money for bad things if they ask for that purpose, but do not withhold money for legitimate goods such as food and housing, even if you suspect they will misuse it. After all, our Father in heaven gives us our bodies, our souls, our health, and all our abilities knowing full well that we will often misuse through sin these very gifts he intends for our welfare. Yet he is still generous to us, hoping that one day we will remember his generosity and return to him. We should do the same with our own children.

So off goes the son, and since he does not have his father's prudence, he squanders his inheritance on his passions. Soon there comes a great famine over the land, something that the son in his imprudence did not foresee. And the son is now destitute. Off he goes to find what work he can, and the only job available is feeding swine, an unclean animal most odious to Jews. But though the son is starving, the owner of the swine doesn't even give him the food that the swine could eat. And so the sweet yoke of paternal authority is fully exchanged—for the harsh yoke of servitude under a master who cares for him less than for his pigs. This is the fate of those who insist that they will not serve, that they will not be subject. They become subject to another anyway, but one who is harder to endure than the master they sought to flee. If we refuse to be slaves of Christ, we shall be made slaves of sin.

Now it happens that when we are filled with emotional satisfaction and feel good, we rarely stop to deliberate and think about what we are doing or where we are going. We just assume that because we feel good, we are doing the right thing and on the road to lasting happiness. So this condition of satisfaction is perhaps the most dangerous of all. If while in this state we are progressing not toward true happiness, but rather toward ruin, we will keep going along that wide and easy road to our demise. On the other hand, when we find ourselves in misery and suffering, we are immediately aware that something is wrong and needs to be fixed or addressed. This is the work of divine justice in our soul: it makes us aware that we are walking along the wrong path.

And so it happens here in this parable: the famine and the want of the prodigal son is God's justice lifting the veil from his eyes, manifesting to him that he has sinned and is on the way to damnation. And because of this gift of God, the son at once begins to deliberate and think over what he has done wrong. This is expressed in the parable by the words *returning to himself.* When we suffer when we experience our misery, we return to our true selves. And what is the first thing that he realizes was false about his past judgments? He realizes that he has misjudged his father; he realizes that his father was really a good man: *How many hired servants in my father's house abound with bread, and here I perish with hunger.*

God's justice has performed the work for which it was intended: it brings an awareness of the constant and enduring goodness of the father in contradistinction to the passing and fallible goodness of the inheritance. It begins to reunite the father with the son, who on account of the love he had for the father's property had separated himself from his father. God the Father treats us in the same way: at the time his wisdom decrees, he begins to take away the things in which we falsely placed our hopes for happiness. And thus does he redirect our hopes from them back to him.

Yet the son still underestimates his father's goodness. He does not believe that his father would simply take him back as his son. In his mind, he thinks that there has to be some reason, some justification, even just a pretext, for his father to take him back. So he begins to formulate an argument by which he hopes to regain his father's good will: *I will arise and go to my father, and say to him: "Father, I have sinned against heaven and before you. I am not worthy to be called your son. Make me as one of your hired servants."* His argument to his father has three statements.

First there is the admission of sin: *I have sinned against heaven, and before you.* Second, there is the assertion of his unworthiness to be taken back: *I am not worthy to be called your son.* Third, there is the suggestion of a punishment: *Make me as one of your hired servants.* Sometimes when we are guilty, we hope to obtain mercy by suggesting our own punishment, and that's what the son does here. His hope at this point is not to be reunited with his father as his son, but merely as his slave. He still vastly underestimates his father's goodness, and is lacking confidence in his father's love for him.

This is how we are too. We sin and realize that we have gravely offended our Father; we know we can't go back to our past sins and keep living that empty life. But in our sense of shame, we cannot believe that our Father would want us as his child. We think that our relationship with God is irreparably damaged by our sinfulness, and we can't go back to being a son the way we were before. And we think we need some argument to be taken back by God: we return to God as to a judge before whom we need a lawyer to argue our case, rather than as to a Father who is happy to see us return. How often in the confessional do penitents spend their time trying to give reasons why God should forgive them, the mitigating circumstances why their sins are not so bad, as if the fact that God is a merciful Father were not a good enough reason!

With his argument in hand, the son begins to carry out the plan he formed: *And rising up he came to his father.* Notice that it says that he came *to his father*, not to his father's house, as if he has begun to realize, however indistinctly, that the important thing is reunion with his father, since he no longer has any hope of being reunited to his father's property. As he makes his way home, St. Luke tells us that *when he was still a long way off, his father saw him.* This implies that the father was actively looking for his son. The son didn't just show up on the doorstep while his father was busy working or attending to something important. No, since the day his son left, the only thing important to him was his son. And so day after day, week after week, month after month, the father sat there on his porch peering with unfounded hope across the horizon to see the sole object of his desire: the return of his son.

How this must have irritated the elder son, seeing his father just a shell of himself, sitting on a rocking chair, doing nothing but looking for that no-good son of his. Jesus is revealing to us what happens in the heart of our heavenly Father when we have sinned. He does not push us out of his mind or forget about us while we are far from him. He does not think about something more important, indifferent to our return. No, when we sin it is as if we are the only thing he can think about; the only object of his desire and longing is to see us return to him. It is as if our Father in heaven is a just a shell of himself until we convert and return to him. Even while we are still far away from God, he looks upon us with his merciful gaze and anticipates our conversion with his grace, and sustains us in our journey back home to him.

When the father saw his son, saw that gait so familiar to a father's eye off in the distance, his heart leaped within him and he *was moved with compassion. And running to him, he fell upon his neck and kissed him.* The first effect of seeing his son return was compassion. He desired to take upon himself all of his son's suffering of the many months he was away. He saw his poor and tattered clothing, his emaciated frame, his dirty feet, his calloused hands, and in an instant he experienced in himself all the suffering of his son. And so he ran to his son—though it is not easy for old men to run—and like a child fell upon his neck and kissed him, weeping. How intensely did the father want his son to know the depth of his love. The father does not humiliate his son; he does not bring up his past transgressions; he does not say "I told you so!" This is how true mercy shows itself: it ennobles and confers dignity, it does not humiliate. St. Maximus the Confessor has a beautiful passage in a letter where he describes this authentic mercy:

> [Jesus] told of how that father, who is goodness itself, was moved with pity for his profligate son who returned and made amends by repentance; how he embraced him, dressed him once more in the fine garments that befitted his own dignity, and did not reproach him for any of his sins. So too, when he found wandering in the mountains and hills the one sheep that had strayed from God's flock of a hundred, he brought it back to the fold but he did not exhaust it by driving it ahead of him. Instead, he placed it on his own shoulders and so compassionately he restored it safely to the flock.[35]

This is how God forgives us when we sincerely repent. He does not humiliate us, he does not even permit us to bring up our past sins, but he lifts us up and ennobles us.

But even with all this, the son goes into his pre-rehearsed argument—he still doubts his father's love! The son says to him: *Father, I have sinned against heaven and before you. I am not now worthy to be called your son.* Recall that before he had intended to say three things: (1) *Father I have sinned against heaven and before you*; (2) *I am not now worthy to be called your son*; and (3) *Make me as one of your hired servants.* But when he speaks to his father, he only says the first two things he had intended to say.[36] Why is that? Because the father interrupts him. The father was pleased to hear his son admit his sinfulness, for this was true, and it was good for his son that he admit it. But he was not pleased to hear him say, "I am not worthy to be called your son," for this was *not true.*

Once a father has begotten a son, that relationship is immutable. Nothing a son can do will change the fact that he is his father's son. So the father is deeply pained to hear his son say he is not worthy to be called his son. The sin of the son does not cause a father's heart to deny him as his son, but rather to convert him from his sin. The father does not want to lose his son, but he wants his son to be loosed from his sin. And so it is with God our Father. Once we have been begotten by him in baptism, we are always his son. By baptism we are incorporated into the eternal sonship of Jesus Christ, and just as his filiation is eternal, so is our filiation immutable. Nothing ever will or ever can change our relationship of sonship to the Father. And if we had committed all the sins from the foundation of the world until today, they would not blot out our filiation. A forgiven son is still a son. And like the prodigal son we can come back to God after our sins and say: "I am not worthy to be called your son." But the Father will say to us in return: "My son, do not say that. You are my son. And you will always be worthy to be called my son."

The inclination to deny the unchangeable reality of our own sonship, to cast off our dignity, is actually Satan's last attempt to render our conversion ineffective. The prodigal wants to come back as a slave to his father; the brothers of Joseph want to come back as slaves to Joseph (Gen. 50:18). So too when we sin we want to come back to the Father not as sons but as slaves, to Jesus not as brothers but as slaves. Satan knows that if we come back to our Father only as a slave, then in our self-loathing he can drive a wedge between us and God again. But self-loathing is not true contrition; it is false contrition since it looks not first to God's goodness, but first to our lack of goodness, which wounds us on account of our pride. Contradicting this spirit of slavery is the spirit of adoption that cries out: "Abba, Father!" (Rom. 8:15).

Seeing that his son still disbelieves his father's love, the father confers upon him all the outward signs of his filial dignity: *"Quickly, bring forth the first robe, and put it on him; and put a ring on his hand, and shoes on his feet. And bring here the fatted calf, and kill it, and let us eat and make merry. Because this, my son, was dead and is come to life again; he was lost and is found." And they began to make merry.* In his body, the prodigal son still bore the outward signs of his servile state, even though in his heart he had received the liberty of sonship. Therefore, in his mercy the father remedies even these outward defects. In exchange for the tattered clothes, the son receives the first robe: the robe reserved for the most important person in the family. To adorn his calloused hands, he brings forth the ring that signifies that he bears his father's authority. Upon his dirty feet are placed shoes that signify that he has been lifted up from the earth, and to once again signify that he was not a slave who went barefoot, but was a son in his father's house. And to remedy his emaciated frame, the fatted calf is killed.

All of this is a sign of the future resurrection, when even our outward selves shall be clothed with glory. And the father himself states the reasons for their celebration. First he gives the reason which was a benefit to the son: *My son was dead and is come to life*; second, he gives the reason which was the benefit to the father: *he was lost but now is found. And they began to make merry.* He does not say, "and they made merry," but *they began to make merry*, as if to say they began but will never cease.

But the parable does not end there, for the younger brother should not only be reconciled to his father, but also to his older brother. *Now the elder son was in the field.* He was dutifully working and fulfilling his father's command. But *when he drew near to the house, he heard music and dancing.* There was joy and celebration, but not on his account. This already was a moment of choice for the elder son. He saw that there was rejoicing because of some good that someone else had done. He could choose to rejoice at the good of another, or from envy he could refuse to rejoice at any good not his own. And since envy began to poison his heart, already he begins to separate himself from his father. The fact that his father saw good reason to rejoice was not good enough for him to rejoice as well.

Nor does he even go to his father to ask about the reason for rejoicing. Instead, *he calls one of the servants*, as if by commanding another he could reassure himself that he was superior to others, *and asked what these things meant.* He seeks to be enlightened by one whom he considers his inferior, when he ought to have sought the meaning of joy from his father, who was its cause. *And he said to him: Your brother has come, and your father has killed the fatted calf, because he has received him safe.* The servant spoke truly, but the effect of this truth was not joy, but anger in the heart of the older son: *And he was filled with wrath and would not go in.* Envy matured into wrath, whose fruit is murder: "For everyone who hates his brother is a murderer" (1 John 3:15). Seeing that the cause of joy was the return of his younger brother, the older brother is filled with wrath, and on account of his wrath he will not go into his father's house.

So now the roles have reversed. Before, out of hatred for his father and love for his father's property, the younger son departed from his father's house, but now out of hatred for his brother, the older son would not enter his father's house. In both cases, the son has become estranged from his father.

Once again, therefore, the father begins to exercise his mercy, this time toward his older son. *His father coming out began to entreat him.* The father was not obliged to respond to his son's unreasonable and childish reaction, yet in his mercy he comes out to him too, and does not rebuke him but pleads with him, entreats him. The parable reveals that all have need of mercy, both the profligate and the obedient. The son's heart is not softened by the father's mildness, but he stubbornly clings to his anger: *Look, for so many years I am serving you, and I have never transgressed your commandment. And yet you have never given me a young goat to make merry with my friends. But as soon as this, your son, is come, who has devoured his substance with harlots you killed for him the fatted calf.* Notice that he calls his younger brother *your son* rather than "my brother." For he has rejected his brother, and in the process unwittingly has denied his own sonship as well by rejecting his father.

I teach logic, and for years I remember reading this argument of the older son and thought to myself: "His argument makes some sense." It goes like this: I was good and he was bad. Now justice demands that you reward the good and punish the bad, but instead you rewarded him and not me. Therefore, you are unjust and I am right to be angry. Seems like a pretty good argument, doesn't it? But attend carefully to the father's response: *Son, you are always with me, and all I have is yours.*

For years I did not understand the importance of that simple phrase: "Son, you are always with me." Yet in it is contained the key to the whole parable. The father is saying to his son: "You claim that you were never rewarded, but all this time you have been together with your father who loves you; was this not enough of a reward for you? Why do you care about a goat? Why do you care so much about my property? And all this time your brother was apart from his loving father. Was this not enough of a punishment for him?" Then the father goes on to show that even with regard to his property he has done no injury to the older brother: *all that I have is yours*, he says. If it's just the property you are interested in rather than being together with your father, then you will inherit all of it, so you have no right to complain.

So you see, it turns out that the older son has the same problem that the younger son had at the beginning of the parable: he loves his father's goods more than his father.

The younger son has been freed of this misery by the loss of his inheritance. He has nothing left but his father. And sometimes that is the most beautiful thing about the loss of created goods we suffer as a punishment for our faults: it leaves us with no one but God to cling to. Mary Magdalene had nothing left of her reputation; there was no pretending anymore that she was good, and she had nothing left to fall back upon, so with all her heart she clung to Christ. So it is okay if we have lost everything. The priest who has been guilty of abuse or some serious crime has lost his right to publicly represent Christ and the Church as a priest. He may even end up in prison. He has lost his inheritance, but he has not lost the possibility of an intimate relationship with his Father. And the same is true of anyone who has committed a very serious sin: perhaps it means losing your job, your freedom, even your family; but you are never stripped of your dignity as a child of your Father. If anything, losing all those created goods finally leaves you no option but God. And how good God is to take us back even when he was our last option. His love for us conquers his own self-respect.

This problem of loving the created goods more than the Father who created them is a problem all of us have. We prefer creatures to the Creator; we identify abundance of created goods with an abundance of God's love. A gift, to be sure, is a sign of love; but as St. Thomas says, love has the notion of the first gift, since all other gifts are given on account of love.[37] And since the gift is better known to us, we confuse the gift with the love, and we come to prefer the gift over the giver of the gift.

But living in a relationship like that eventually brings sadness and disappointment. There are many cases of young people from wealthy families whose father left their mother and married another woman; and in some attempt to make it up to their children, he showers them with expensive presents: a nice car when they turn sixteen, an exotic trip when they graduate, and so on. But as this goes on the children become more and more demanding of things, and at the same time become more and more resentful of their father. They see him as merely something to be used, and this kind of relationship with one's own father ultimately leads to self-loathing. In the depths of their being, they need to be united with their father as a person to have a sense of their own dignity, while in their outward acts they treat him as a tool, as something without dignity. So they lose the sense of their own dignity.

Our Father in heaven is not about to let that happen to us. He will not continue to shower us with gifts and let us lose the sense of our dignity as his children. In fact, no creature is adequate to manifest his love for us, so at some point, at least at the moment of our death (if not sooner), he removes from us every created good so that we will not think that his love is only as great as the goodness we find in some creature. Our whole life is a training ground in which God gradually takes from us the created goods we depend on, like training wheels on our bicycle, until at the end of our lives we can face the loss of everything, even life itself, with confidence in our Father's love for us. Eventually, we have to stand face to face not with the gift, but with the love of the Giver, which exceeds all gifts. This is what St. John of the Cross refers to when he says we have to come to the point where we have nothing, nothing, nothing.

Priests need to help people see the primacy of the relationship with the Father. And the first, best way to do this is for a priest to be completely *toward the Father*. The priest of Jesus Christ must be free from the desire to find fulfillment in creatures, and must instead have always before his eyes the Father as the sole object of his love. Only then can our witness to others, especially penitents, be authentic. Our mercy in the confessional will reflect the mercy of the Father if we help the repentant sinner see that it is union with the Father that matters, not the many things of this world that we fear to lose.

Sometimes it happens that after a particularly shameful fall, a repentant sinner realizes that he deserves to lose everything he holds dear: his family, his priestly office, or whatever. Yet since the sin is hidden or at least not yet known by others, the possibility of keeping those created goods remains. So he clings to the misguided hope that he can keep these created goods, like a man clinging to what's left of his cargo after a shipwreck. Someone in this condition must be reassured that it's okay to let go. Just swim to shore where you will be safe, and don't risk drowning for the sake of some created good you think is necessary to be happy. If God thinks it will help you to be happy, it will wash up on shore, but let him decide that. Perhaps God will allow you to keep those things, perhaps not. In fact, there may be good reasons not to reveal the sin for the sake of the common good; but interiorly the repentant sinner needs to let go of his dependence upon those created goods if he is ever to find peace. Otherwise, he will constantly live in fear of his sin becoming known, and that kind of fear makes us the plaything of the devil.

After showing his older son why he should not be angry, the father concludes by explaining to his son why he should rejoice: *It was fitting that that we should make merry and be glad, for this, your brother, was dead and is come to life again; he was lost and is found.* He calls him *your brother*, not "my son," to manifest to him that it is to his good, too, that the younger son came home. To have a brother is to have a very great good, for a brother is of the same parents, and it is the greatest good that parents can give to their child. For each new sibling is a renewal of the love between the father and mother, and so it manifests to the children that their parents love one another. And peace and joy reign in the hearts of children.

We too ought to rejoice in the good of our brother, especially his repentance. For when our brother has been brought to life again, this act of spiritual regeneration is not only a good for the one reborn, but also a sign to us of the love that our Father has for us. And it is also a sign of the love of our mother Mary for us, since she cooperates with the Holy Spirit to bring about this rebirth in our brother. How good it is to know that Mary our mother is loved by God and loves God. This brings peace and joy to our souls.

The Spiritual Sense of the Parable: Jesus as the Prodigal Son

Like so many of our Lord's parables, the parable of the prodigal son can be read on many different levels. When this parable is read in Greek, it becomes abundantly clear that one way to read the parable is to understand that the prodigal son is Jesus. At the beginning of the parable, it says that the prodigal son asks for the *ousias* (literally, the "substance") of the father, and that the father gives him his *bion* (literally, his "life"). Jesus is the Son who is consubstantial with the Father, who shares a single life with his Father. At the moment of the Incarnation, the Son takes the substance of the Father into a far-off land, that is, into creation, which is infinitely distant from the Creator. And this happens *not many days later*, since creation was completed on the seventh day, after which Christ came into the world. He squanders all he has especially on sinners and prostitutes, since Christ gave from the fullness of his grace to men: "Of his fullness we have all received" (John 1:16).

This is called *squandering* since the divine gifts are superabundant and not capable of being grasped fully by any creature, so that always more is given than can be received. *And when all things had been consumed*, by revealing the fullness of divine truth and manifesting the abundance of divine love for men, Jesus handed himself over to his Passion and death, which is described as a *great famine*. This moment is described in St. John's Gospel where it says, "Jesus, knowing that all was now consummated" (John 19:28). And he was longing to be filled with our love, but *no one gave him anything*. For in their condition as creatures, men were not able to give anything to Christ unless he first gave to men, as St. Paul teaches: "What have you that you have not received?" (1 Cor. 4:7).

After describing his Passion and death, the parable describes his Resurrection. Hence, it continues: *having come into himself*—that is, by his Resurrection—*he said, "How many of my Father's hired servants are abounding in bread?"* In fact, none were abounding in the bread of life until Christ should rise again, so if they were to abound in the life-giving Eucharist, he would have to rise from the dead. Finally, Christ resolves to ascend to the Father: "Having risen" (*anastas*, literally "having resurrected"), he says, *I shall go toward my Father.* And he does this so that we might "seek the things that are above, where Christ is, seated at the right hand of God."[38] In Jesus Christ, the Father receives all poor sinners who are united to him by love, and he glorifies us as he glorifies his Son at the Ascension. And at the end of time, the heavenly banquet shall begin but never end because *my Son was dead and came to life again; he was lost and was found.*

Even read merely as a piece of literature, the parable of the prodigal son is starkly beautiful. But when read as the word of God, it bears the power of eternal salvation to those who read it with an open heart.

Joseph and the Prodigal Son

In the background of the parable of the prodigal son is the life of the patriarch Joseph, one of the twelve sons of Jacob. There can be no doubt that Jesus intended us to compare the life of Joseph to the prodigal son. Consider these parallels between their stories:

- Both the prodigal son and Joseph had envious older brothers (Gen. 37:1–11).

- Both the prodigal son and Joseph leave their father and go to a far-off land where there is a famine (Gen. 41:54–57).

- Both are tempted to be intimate with women (Gen. 39:7).

- Both are temporarily enslaved in the far-off land (Gen. 39:20).

- Both receive a special robe from their father (Gen. 37:3).

- Both receive a ring (Gen. 41:42).

- Both are presumed dead by their father, but found alive (Gen. 45:28).

- Both are reunited with their father by an embrace and a kiss. In fact, nearly the same words are used to recount both reunions: "Then Joseph made ready his chariot and went up to meet Israel his father in Goshen; and he presented himself to him, and *fell on his neck*, and wept on his neck a good while" (Gen. 46:29).

That's not just three or four parallels—that's at least eight! There are so many exact parallels that one cannot doubt that our Lord intended for us to consider his parable side by side with the story of Joseph. But in spite of the parallels, the differences are also striking:

- The prodigal son departs willingly; Joseph departs unwillingly.

- The prodigal son hungers from famine; Joseph feeds others during the famine.

- The prodigal son is a slave until he returns home; Joseph is made second in the kingdom while in that far-off land.

- The prodigal son receives a robe on his return home, Joseph before his departure.

- The prodigal son receives a ring from his father, but Joseph receives a ring from Pharaoh.

- The prodigal son is intimate with women; Joseph resists the advances of a woman.

- The prodigal son is embraced by his father; Joseph embraces his father.

- The prodigal son returns to his father in his original home; Joseph brings his father and his entire family into that far-off land.

What does this all mean? Christ is the key that unlocks all of Scripture. Both Joseph and the prodigal son represent Christ. But since Christ has both a human and a divine origin, being Son of Man and Son of God, the same story is told from the perspective of each. Fittingly, the Old Testament tells the story from the perspective of Christ's human origin, whereas the New Testament tells the same story from the perspective of Christ's divine origin. Let us see how each reflects the life of Christ.

The father in the history of Joseph represents Adam, the human origin of Christ, and from the beginning Christ is clothed with the robe of human nature upon coming into the world at the Incarnation. As man he takes no wife, resisting the inclination of human nature to be joined to a woman. He departs this world unwillingly at his Passion, crying out "Father, if it be possible, let this chalice pass from me" (Luke 22:42). But he enters into the next life, a land far from this. He dwells in prison there only for a short time, for "he went and preached to the spirits in prison" (1 Pet. 3:19). Then, at his Resurrection and Ascension, he is raised up to the right hand of the throne of God the Father.

For in the story of Joseph, Pharaoh represents God the Father. Thus, the ring given to Joseph by Pharaoh symbolizes the eternal divinity and its union with Christ's humanity, since a ring is circular, having no beginning or end, signifying eternity. And just as Pharaoh makes Joseph second in the

kingdom, yet in such a way that he exercises the full authority of the King, so too does God the Father establish Christ
at his right hand, exercising his full authority. From there
Christ feeds hungry souls with bread from heaven, nourish-
ing them with his own glorious flesh and blood. Finally,
he welcomes tearful Adam with an embrace and a kiss, and
leads Adam and all his children into heaven.

The father in the parable of the prodigal son is God the
Father. His homeland signifies heaven, while the far-off
land signifies this fallen world. Christ willingly departs from
his heavenly home so that he might come to save us here in
this fallen world, so far off from heaven. Upon coming into
the world, Christ hungers and thirsts, experiencing famine
while he lives in the "likeness of sinful flesh" (Rom. 8:3).
He spends all and, in his divinity, he draws near to prostitutes and sinners, allowing them to be intimate with him in
supernatural love. But having emptied himself and having
taken "the form of a slave" (Phil. 2:7), he subjected himself to the slavery of death, he rises up[39] again and returns
to his Father, receiving the glorious robe of his resurrected
body together with a ring that signifies the manifestation of
his eternal divinity. He is welcomed by his Father into his
original, heavenly home, where he shall forever rejoice in
the heavenly banquet.

There is some question about who the envious older
brothers represent in each story. In the story of Joseph, it
seems that the envious older brothers are the leaders of the
Jewish people: "he perceived that it was out of envy that
the chief priests had delivered him up" (Mark 15:10). In the
story of the prodigal son, I think the envious older brother can represent the devil. The scriptures tell us that the
devil was envious (Wis. 2:24).[40] But how can he be called
older than the divine Word, since the Word existed before

all creatures? Because he is old not in time, but in sin (see Dan. 13:52), which is why St. Paul calls the man subject to sin the "old man" (Rom. 6:6). Again, because the divine Word is eternally begotten of the Father, his begetting is eternally new: "This day I have begotten you" (Acts 13:33; Heb. 1:5; 5:5). And just as one who is further from birth is called older, so too all creatures are old in comparison to the Word who is eternally, newly begotten.

So there you have it. It is the same story. Sacred Scripture is truly miraculous. It is the word of God.

Being Evangelized by the Parable of the Prodigal Son

Who are you in this parable? Are you the younger son who wants to be free from the burden of serving God your Father? Or are you that same younger son who doubts that his Father wants him back after his sins? Or are you the elder son who cares more about his friends and goats than about his relationship with his Father? Often enough we are all of these at some point in our lives. And regardless of where we are in our own spiritual lives, there is the same remedy for our problems: to recognize the primacy of our relationship with our Father. We must always and everywhere be wholly toward our Father.

Evangelizing by Means of the Parable of the Prodigal Son

Our purpose in evangelizing is to "turn the hearts of the children toward their Father" (Mal. 4:6). So we need to determine where someone stands in relation to his Father. If he is the rebellious younger son, we should ask him why he thinks the inheritance will make him happy; why he thinks it will be a sufficient substitute for the love of his Father.

Others we meet will be like the broken-down son, having experienced the disappointment of being let down by the inheritance, the goods of this world, yet fearful that his Father does not want him back. To such a person, this parable is a reminder of the Father's firm and unchangeable love. We should point out the many signs of the Father's love for them, especially the sacrament of penance. Finally, we will encounter others like the older son, who feel the burden of the commandments and yet feel unrewarded and unappreciated. To these we must repeat the words of the Father in the parable: "Son, you are always with me." We must try to open their eyes to the greatest good that they possess in keeping the commandments: union with their Father who loves them.

CHAPTER 13

JESUS AND PETER ON THE BEACH

The last conversation I want to consider is that between Jesus and Peter on the beach after the Resurrection. It is the encounter of every sinner with Christ after his repentance.

When they had finished breakfast, Jesus said to Simon Peter, "Simon, son of John, do you love me more than these?" He said to him, "Yes, Lord, you know that I love you." He said to him, "Feed my lambs." He then said to him a second time, "Simon, son of John, do you love me?" He said to him, "Yes, Lord, you know that I love you." He said to him, "Tend my sheep." He said to him the third time, "Simon, son of John, do you love me?" Peter was distressed that he had said to him a third time, "Do you love me?" and he said to him, "Lord, you know everything; you know that I love you."

[Jesus] said to him, "Feed my sheep. Amen, amen, I say to you, when you were younger, you used to dress yourself and go where you wanted; but when you grow old, you will stretch out your hands, and someone else will dress you and lead you where you do not want to go." He said this signifying by what kind of death he would glorify God. And when he had said this, he said to him, "Follow me." Peter turned and saw the disciple following whom Jesus loved, the one who had also reclined upon his chest during the supper and had said, "Master, who is the one who will betray you?" When Peter saw him, he said to Jesus, "Lord, what about him?" Jesus said to him, "What if I want him to remain until I come? What concern is it of yours? You follow me" (John 21:15–22).

The Context of the Conversation

The setting is telling. Chapter twenty-one begins with Peter going out to fish with some of the other apostles. They fish all night and catch nothing, and then Jesus appears in the early morning on the shore and tells them to cast the net on the other side, and they take in a miraculous catch. All this hearkens back to Peter's original call to follow Jesus, when at first he had said "depart from me for I am a sinful man" (Luke 5:8). But now Peter jumps in the water and swims toward the Lord. At the beginning of his vocation Peter wanted to flee from Jesus out of fear, but now he longs to be united with Jesus out of love.

The Meaning of the Conversation: Peter Relives His Entire Vocation

The verses that follow continue to recapitulate Peter's entire vocational history. Peter hauls in the fish, symbolizing his apostolic labors during the three years of following the Lord; he dines with Jesus, symbolizing the Last Supper; and after they dine they have this conversation on the shore, next to a charcoal fire.[41] This recalls and recapitulates the events of the Passion between the Last Supper and the Resurrection. If we read carefully, it is as if Peter's vocation is being re-wound: played again backward. The shore upon which Jesus now stands is the firm and certain shore of eternal life, the shore on the other side of the sea. So instead of ending with the Resurrection, this part of Peter's vocation begins with the Resurrection.

The charcoal fire has been lit to remind Peter of the place where he had denied Christ three times (John 21:9). Three times Peter had denied Christ from fear near a charcoal fire; three times he must profess him in love near a charcoal fire. All of this is untying the knots by which Peter had bound his own soul. Even the conversation that Jesus and Peter have on the beach is a replay of the conversation Jesus and Peter had on the same subjects before the Passion:

> Jesus said to them: "You will all fall away because of me this night; for it is written, 'I will strike the shepherd, and the sheep of the flock will be scattered.' But after I am raised up, I will go before you to Galilee." Peter declared to him: "Though they all fall away because of you, I will never fall away." Jesus said to him: "Truly I say to you, this very night, before the cock crows, you will deny me three times." Peter said to him: "Even if I must die with you, I will not deny you" (Matt. 26:31–35).

All the same subjects come up: Peter loving Jesus more than the others; Peter following Jesus even unto death; the shepherd; the sheep. In that earlier conversation, Jesus had some very bleak and sad things to say on those subjects. The shepherd will be struck; the sheep scattered and shepherd-less; Peter denying Jesus, loving Jesus even less than the others. Jesus foretold a tragedy, but Peter wrote his own script with a happy ending. Peter wanted a heroic epic in which he played the lead role. We know, of course, how things turned out.

Peter's tragic flaw was that he presumed to know himself better than Jesus knew him. It is this flaw that Jesus comes to heal some weeks later when the Lord resumes their conversation that had been interrupted by the Passion. Most English translations do not quite capture the nuances of the Greek text.[42] If we were to read it in Greek, the conversation would sound more like this:

> Jesus: *Do you love me with an all-consuming love, more than the others?*
>
> Peter: *I love you as a friend.*
>
> Jesus: *Do you at least love me with an all-consuming love?*
>
> Peter: *I love you as a friend.*
>
> Jesus: *Do you even love me as a friend?*
>
> Peter: [You can almost sense the sadness and uncertainty in his voice as he says] *Lord, you know all things, you know whether or not I even love you as a friend.*

In so many ways the scene is pathetic. Peter has come to grips with the fact that he does not even know for certain what is in his own heart—only Jesus can tell him. Peter is shaken, broken. Gone is the bravado, gone the false certainty, gone the empty boasts. Yet even as Peter lets go of all hope in his own ability to love and follow Jesus, to fulfill the mission entrusted to him by Jesus, Jesus himself promises that Peter will indeed accomplish all those things he once thought he could do on his own. But the power now belongs to Jesus, so that Peter might have a hope founded upon the promise and the power of Christ rather than upon his own empty boasts.

In this passage Jesus reverses all of Peter's failings through-out his entire vocation. He reverses the effects of all his sins, his lies, his fears, his sorrows. Every evil in Peter's life is turned into something good and holy. It is not just that Jesus ignores Peter's past and gives him a fresh start. No, he takes Peter back through his life and transforms each failure in Peter's past into something beautiful. Nothing was wasted, not even Peter's sins: "all things work together for good for those who love God, who are called according to his pur-pose" (Rom. 8:28). It was necessary for the Lord to bring Peter along this path so that he might care for the lambs and the sheep of the Lord's fold. Peter was to serve in place of the Lord, so he had to be a docile instrument in the hand of the Lord, not someone who ruled the sheep for his own purposes: "Do not lord it over those assigned to you, but be examples to the flock. And when the chief Shepherd is revealed, you will receive the unfading crown of glory" (1 Pet. 5:3–4).

Being Evangelized by the Conversation with Peter on the Beach

Our own lives, our own vocations, tend to mirror that of Peter. We begin with so many dreams—we write our own script, we make ourselves the hero. Yet despite our lip-service to God's grace, for the most part we have tried to fashion our lives and our vocations according to our own likings, our own preconceptions about how things should turn out. And to the degree we continue to insist on making our own happy ending by our own choices and abilities and talents, on reinventing our lives and our vocations, we have not yet learned the lesson of this Gospel.

For most of us it is true: until we have experienced what it means to utterly fail, we do not know the extent to which we should mistrust our own abilities and talents; so we have not yet begun to follow Christ. If it is Jesus' will for us, it is better to be the biggest failure, to live in uncertainty about our love and fidelity to Christ, to be the one who loves Jesus the least, than to live in a self-created world of imagined love and false glory. Jesus has the power to turn our failures and misery to his own purposes, and once our hope is founded entirely upon his power, we can, for the first time, begin to follow Jesus.

Evangelizing by Means of the Conversation with Peter on the Beach

More than anything, this conversation is a means for evangelizing the failed apostle: the person who strove to be faithful to Jesus, yet at the crucial moment fell on account of his weakness; the person who has tried to bring souls to Christ but has had little success. Everyone sent by the Lord is weak and prone to failure because of hidden pride. Yet in all this, pride must not have the ultimate victory through discouragement or despair. We must raise up the fallen apostle with hope in the truth that Jesus uses even our sins for his greater glory and for the good of the elect. Conversion turns every defeat into victory: for in our conversion both the power and the mercy of the Lord is revealed. The rolls of the saints are filled with the doubly converted and even with the innumerably converted: those who tried and failed, yet tried one more time than they failed. Once the Lord said that if our brother sins against us seven times in one day, and seven times he be converted, forgive him (Luke 17:4). He will not demand from us more than he is willing to do for us.

The apostle might also suffer from discouragement because of lack of apostolic success. They see that they are not convincing witnesses to the gospel because of their many faults, so they do not see results in their efforts to save souls. Perhaps they have fished all night and caught nothing. But it is easy for the Lord to grant us a miraculous catch at the end, to catch more fish than if we had successfully fished our whole life long. Our duty is simply to keep lowering our nets, to keep trying to serve the Lord who wants us to be faithful despite discouraging results. He it is who brings about conversion, and he will do it in his own time.

The same principle holds true about our own following of the Lord. Perhaps at the end of our life, the Lord will grant a miraculous catch of his grace. It is not difficult for the one who converted Saul on the road to Damascus to make us into great saints in a single moment, even with our last breath. None of us runs along the hard and narrow way to heaven, none of us runs while following Christ. Either we limp, or we crawl, or, if we are just humble enough, we are carried in the arms of the Lord.

EPILOGUE

When the Word was made flesh, he dwelt among us in human form, using human words to express the inexpressible truth about God. He planted the seed of his word into human hearts, beginning with the Immaculate Heart of his mother, where he found soil more fertile than the highest heavens. From there he scattered the seed of the word into the hearts of his apostles. They, in turn, bore fruit and planted his word throughout the world, and it has not ceased from that time until now to bear fruit thirty, sixty, and a hundredfold.

This small book is itself the fruit produced from seeds planted by others. And like all fruit, it contains the seed from which it came. It is my hope that the word of God has dwelt in you richly as you have read, prayed, and meditated upon these passages from the Gospels. You too must bear fruit, not only in words, but in deed and truth. May God bless you with an abundant harvest. Amen!

ABOUT THE AUTHOR

Fr. Sebastian Walshe, O. Praem. is a Norbertine canon of the Abbey of St. Michael in the Diocese of Orange, California. After earning a degree in electrical engineering, Fr. Sebastian worked at an intellectual property firm before pursuing further education at Thomas Aquinas College. Graduating in 1994, he continued studies at the Catholic University of America in Washington D.C., receiving a license in philosophy. Later, while in the seminary, he attended the Pontifical University of St. Thomas at Rome (the Angelicum) where he received a master's degree in sacred theology and a doctorate in philosophy. Since 2006, Fr. Sebastian has been a professor of philosophy in the seminary program at St. Michael's Abbey, where he is the dean of studies.

ENDNOTES

1   Taken from the Office of Readings, Memorial of St. John of the Cross, Dec. 14.

2   Prologue to the Commentary on Isaiah.

3   In fact, God frequently offers signs in the future as a reward for faith in the present, as he did with Moses (Exod. 3:12); with Ahaz (Isa. 7:14) and with the Blessed Virgin Mary (Luke 1:36).

4   Hugh of St. Victor, De Arca Noe 2, 8: PL 176, 642 (Cf. CCC 134).

5   Cf. The Interpretation of the Bible in the Church, Pontifical Biblical Commission, Introduction of His Holiness, John Paul II, 6.

6   *On Christian Doctrine*, I.36.

7   This is not to be confused with the distinction between proper and figurative speech. Both proper and figurative speech concerns the meanings of words, and so these both fall under the literal sense. When Jesus says that he is the Son of God, that is proper speech. When Jesus says that he will sit at the right hand of the Father, that is figurative or metaphorical speech. But both are instances of the literal sense of Scripture. On the other hand, when the things signified by the words of Scripture themselves bear a clear meaning, this pertains to a spiritual sense of Scripture.

8   Many Fathers of the Church explained the allegorical sense of the Exodus in similar terms. See, for example, the Catechetical Instructions of St. Cyril of Jerusalem.

9   I have not reproduced the text of Genesis 1 here, but it may be helpful for the reader to read over that chapter in his own Bible together with my explanation. For this particular consideration of the creation story in Genesis, I want to thank my friend Michael Augros who contributed to this exegesis.

10 Commentary on John, chap. 5, lecture 9.

11 *Summa Theologiae*, Ia, q.1, a.9.

12 I have considered some of these "rocks" in the first chapter: for example, doubts about reconciling Scripture with science, doubts about the honesty of the sacred authors, etc.

13 These words, attributed to the Blessed Virgin Mary in one of her apparitions to St. Bernadette, are inscribed around her shrine at the Convent of St. Gildard in Nevers, France.

14 *The Sermons of St. Thomas Aquinas*, Sermon 11, part 3.

15 Pelagians are the followers of Pelagius, a heretic in the early Church. The heresy of Pelagius denied the dogma of original sin and asserted that man could make himself pleasing to God without the assistance of God's grace.

16 The Holy Spirit is called the "finger of God" in Scripture and in Sacred Tradition. Compare, for example, the parallel texts of Luke 11:20 and Matt. 12:28. This is an apt metaphor for the Holy Spirit, since just as a finger proceeds from the hand and arm that proceeds from the body, so too does the Holy Spirit proceed from the Son who is called the "right hand" and "arm" of the Father. Moreover, just as the finger of the artist is what immediately touches his work, so too the Holy Spirit is most intimately present in the soul of believer, God's handiwork.

17 Citation of Isaiah 45:8 taken from the responsorial psalm of Wednesday of the third week of Advent.

18 See Genesis 2:7: "The LORD God formed man out of the clay of the ground and blew into his nostrils the breath of life, and so man became a living being."

19 See Wisdom 18:14–15: "For when peaceful stillness compassed everything and the night in its swift course was half spent, your all-powerful word from heaven's royal throne bounded, a fierce warrior, into the doomed land."

20 This is a traditional understanding based upon the scriptures and the teaching of the Fathers and Doctors of the Church. For example, the prophet Zechariah says about the Lord's coming on the Day of Judgment: "That day his feet shall rest upon the Mount of Olives" (Zech. 14:4); and Thomas Aquinas teaches that "it can be gathered with probability from the scriptures that [the Lord] will descend around the place of the Mount of Olives, just as he ascended from there" (*Commentary on the Sentences*, Bk. IV, q.1, a.4D).

21 *Summa Theologiae*, II–IIae, q.21, a.2.

22 Cf. 2 Cor. 2:14: "But thanks be to God, who always leads us as captives in Christ's triumphal procession and uses us to spread the aroma of the knowledge of him everywhere."

23 See, for example, his admonitions in the introduction to his *Praxis Confessarii*.

24 Sermon 46.

25 St. Augustine, Ev. l., ii, q.19.

26 St. Theopylactus, Homily on Luke, ch. 10.

27 *Summa Theologiae*, IIIa, q.61, a.1.

28 From the *Spiritual Testament of St. Bernadette.*

29 Sermon 43.

30 "There are different kinds of spiritual gifts but the same Spirit; there are different forms of service but the same Lord; there are different workings but the same God who produces all of them in everyone. To each individual the manifestation of the Spirit is given for some benefit" (1 Cor. 12:4–7).

31 "The garden of the Lord, brethren, includes—yes, it truly includes—not only the roses of martyrs but also the lilies of virgins, and the ivy of married people, and the violets of widows" (St. Augustine, Sermon 304, 14, PL 38).

32 *Diary of St. Faustina* 1017.

33 It seems to me that the inability to see this truth is one of the marks of scrupulosity. The scrupulous person is obsessed with avoiding evil, even if this means omitting great good. For example, he will omit receiving Communion out of fear of sacrilege, even if there is little evidence that he has sinned gravely. For the scrupulous person, God is a harsh master to be defended against by means of a contract, not a generous father who is to be approached with confidence and gratitude. For the scrupulous person, salvation is not joy, but merely relief.

34 See John 6:64, 6:71, and Luke 22:21, which imply that Judas betrayed Jesus because he refused to believe in the real presence of our Lord in the Eucharist.

35 Epistle 11: PG 91, 454-455.

36 There are some manuscripts in which the third statement is also found here, but the best texts omit the third statement. The manuscripts that include it can be explained by copyists who assumed it was left out by the mistake of an earlier copyist and so inserted the third statement from earlier in the parable.

37 *Summa Theologiae*, Ia, q.38, a.2.

38 Colossians 3:1.

39 The Greek word used in the parable when the prodigal son "rose up" is the same word used to signify Christ's Resurrection.

40 The envy of the devil was probably on account of the fact that God had become man.

41 See John 21:9.

42 Some Greek Fathers, such as St. John Chrysostom, treat the two Greek words *agapas* and *phileis* as interchangeable, so perhaps we should not make too much of this distinction. Nevertheless, both Augustine and St. Thomas point out that the words are different and even have a difference in meaning (see, for example, St. Thomas's commentary on John 21), so the sacred author is trying to communicate something by this difference.